Local Economic and Employment Development

Flexible Policy for More and Better Jobs

Edited by Sylvain Giguère and Francesca Froy

OECD

ORGANISATION FOR ECONOMIC CO-OPERATION AND DEVELOPMENT

The OECD is a unique forum where the governments of 30 democracies work together to address the economic, social and environmental challenges of globalisation. The OECD is also at the forefront of efforts to understand and to help governments respond to new developments and concerns, such as corporate governance, the information economy and the challenges of an ageing population. The Organisation provides a setting where governments can compare policy experiences, seek answers to common problems, identify good practice and work to co-ordinate domestic and international policies.

The OECD member countries are: Australia, Austria, Belgium, Canada, the Czech Republic, Denmark, Finland, France, Germany, Greece, Hungary, Iceland, Ireland, Italy, Japan, Korea, Luxembourg, Mexico, the Netherlands, New Zealand, Norway, Poland, Portugal, the Slovak Republic, Spain, Sweden, Switzerland, Turkey, the United Kingdom and the United States. The Commission of the European Communities takes part in the work of the OECD.

OECD Publishing disseminates widely the results of the Organisation's statistics gathering and research on economic, social and environmental issues, as well as the conventions, guidelines and standards agreed by its members.

This work is published on the responsibility of the Secretary-General of the OECD. The opinions expressed and arguments employed herein do not necessarily reflect the official views of the Organisation or of the governments of its member countries.

About the Authors

Randall Eberts is Executive Director of the W.E. Upjohn Institute for Employment Research, an independent non-profit research organisation that conducts and supports research on policy-relevant employment and regional economic issues. His current research examines the role of local partnerships in workforce and economic development. Mr. Eberts also works closely with the federal and state governments to develop management tools that use statistical analysis to help improve the performance of workforce programmes. He received his Ph.D. in economics from Northwestern University.

Francesca Froy is a Senior Policy Analyst within Local Economic and Employment Development (LEED) at the OECD where she co-ordinates activities relating to employment, skills and local governance. She implements studies on Managing Accountability and Flexibility, Skills for Competitiveness and Integrating Employment, Skills and Economic Development and also co-edited the OECD publication "*From Immigration to Integration: Local Solutions to a Global Challenge*". Prior to joining LEED she helped to manage the DG Employment and Social Affairs initiative IDELE (identification and dissemination of local employment development). An anthropologist by background, she has worked for a number of years in both the Public Employment Service and a municipal government in the United Kingdom.

Sylvain Giguère is Head of the Local Economic and Employment Development (LEED) Division at the OECD. He manages a team of economists, analysts and support staff based at both the OECD Headquarters in Paris and the OECD LEED Centre for Local Development in Trento, Italy. A Canadian national, Mr. Giguère joined the OECD in 1995 and developed a policy research agenda to provide guidance on how public policies can be better co-ordinated and adapted to local conditions to improve economic and social outcomes. This work has produced a broad range of policy lessons, from labour market policy to economic development, published widely. He studied economics at University of Quebec in Montreal and Queen's University (Kingston, Ont.) and holds a Ph.D. in economics from University of Paris 1 (Sorbonne).

Hugh Mosley is Senior Research Fellow in the Labour Market and Employment Research Unit at the Social Research Centre (WZB) in Berlin where he has worked since 1986. His recent work has been on implementation issues, especially on public employment service reforms, and on policy evaluation. Hugh has published extensively in specialised journals and advises the European Commission and the OECD on labour market policy. His current work focuses on the evaluation of the Hartz labour market reforms in Germany for the German Ministry of Labour.

Dave Simmonds OBE is the co-founder and Chief Executive of the Centre for Economic and Social Inclusion. Dave has been involved in social exclusion, labour market and regeneration policy for the last 22 years, both in policy formulation and practical implementation. He has advised government and social partners on welfare reform and the delivery of support to unemployed people. He previously worked as Director of Policy for the UK National Council for Voluntary Organisations.

FLEXIBLE POLICY FOR MORE AND BETTER JOBS – ISBN 978-92-64-05918-4 – © OECD 2009

Foreword

Two ministerial conferences have been held over a 10-year interval – in 1998 and 2008 – in Venice, Italy on the theme of decentralising labour market policy. Both events, hosted by the Italian Minister of Labour, gathered ministers from OECD member and non member countries in addition to a large number of high-level officials. This is a demonstration of the sustained interest that exists on the issue of decentralisation and devolution in the area of employment and skills development.

To respond to this high level of interest, the LEED Directing Committee has been working on a far reaching research agenda in the area of employment and governance. This agenda has examined the experience of OECD countries in decentralising policies, establishing area-based partnerships and new forms of governance, setting up initiatives to upgrade the skills of the low-qualified and integrate immigrants, co-ordinating workforce and economic development policies, and designing integrated skills development strategies locally. The results, published in a dozen reports, have generated policy recommendations that have proved critical in responding to the challenge of improving prosperity for all in a global economy through better functioning labour markets.

Our publication More than Just Jobs: Workforce Development in a Skills-based Economy, released for the 2008 conference, summarised some of the main lessons for policy and practice stemming from this work agenda. One of the lessons stands above the others: making labour market policy and training more flexible and adaptable locally. This is the surest way to act decisively on two crucial issues: helping workers progress in employment; and upgrading local labour and skills demand by assisting productivity enhancement in enterprises.

The issue of flexibility in the management of labour market policy, discussed in depth during the 2008 Venice conference, held with the support of Isfol and Italia Lavoro, is the main subject of this volume. For the first time, it presents estimates of the degree of flexibility allowed at various governance levels in OECD countries, and compares results across countries. It assesses the most direct impacts of flexibility on employment outcomes, identifies the most important challenges in balancing flexibility against accountability, and provides concrete examples of initiatives and results achieved.

The content of this publication holds a particular political importance in that it underpins a commitment made by the labour ministers and senior officials in Venice.

At the conference, the participants adopted the Venice Action Statement, which lists a series of action to take to move forward on the agenda of improving quality employment today (see Annex A to this publication). The main recommendations agreed include injecting flexibility in the management of labour market policy, fostering partnerships, supporting local intelligence and building capacities.

This book will play a special role in the implementation of this agreed policy agenda for governments in OECD member and non member countries. It also launches a second phase of policy research as part of LEED's work agenda on employment and governance. It is my hope that its guidance to governments will prove as useful as the outputs from our previous phases of research.

Sergio Arzeni
Director, OECD Centre for Entrepreneurship
SMEs and Local Development.

Acknowledgments.   Sylvain Giguère, Head, and Francesca Froy, Senior Policy Analyst, at the OECD Programme on Local Economic and Employment Development (LEED) prepared and edited this publication. Debbie Binks, Sheelagh Delf, Lucy Clarke and Damian Garnys should be thanked for their administrative and technical support.

The editors would like to thank Randall Eberts, Hugh Mosley and Dave Simmonds for their generous contributions. We would also like to thank our colleagues in the Directorate for Employment, Labour and Social Affairs for their significant collaboration, support and advice at various stages in the project, and in particular David Grubb, Paul Swaim and Peter Tergeist.

Table of Contents

List of Boxes

List of Tables

List of Figures

FLEXIBLE POLICY FOR MORE AND BETTER JOBS – ISBN 978-92-64-05918-4 – © OECD 2009

ISBN 978-92-64-05918-4
Flexible Policy for More and Better Jobs
© OECD 2009

Executive Summary

In the context of globalisation and rapid technological progress, human resources and skills are becoming increasingly crucial to economic development. This is especially pressing in the aftermath of the global economic slowdown. Labour market agencies and institutions have the capacity to contribute significantly to returning localities to prosperity, but only if they adapt themselves to new priorities: helping workers to compete on the global market, and helping regions to move along the path towards a high-skills, high-productivity equilibrium.

The current global economic context calls for more intelligence gathering, more partnership building, and more strategic thinking. It is not just employment agencies that are required to act. In order to be effective they need to work with other stakeholders, particularly in the areas of economic development and vocational training. Policy strands need to be well co-ordinated and adapted to meet local challenges. Local agencies also need to look to the future – the most competitive local labour force will be one that has the generic skills required to adapt to change as it occurs and keep pace with new economic opportunities.

Such local activism does not always fit with the standardised procedures of employment and training organisations. Public employment services are often managed in a relatively centralised fashion, offering few possibilities for local agencies to identify for themselves the opportunities to be seized and the problems to be tackled. The demand for more proactive local employment agencies has significant implications for how government policies are designed and managed, with one of the biggest challenges being to provide more flexibility on the ground where policies are implemented. Ministers and high level officials at an OECD conference in Venice on 17-19 April 2008 agreed that it essentially requires a new framework for the management of workforce development (see Annex A, "Venice Action Statement").

Some of these issues have caused analysts and politicians to press for a greater decentralisation of labour market policy and, in particular, for devolution to regions. Yet our analysis shows that the formal distribution of power is less important than the actual flexibility available to actors at different levels within the system – local, sub-regional, regional and national. By flexibility we mean here the possibility to adjust policy at its various design, implementation and delivery stages to make it better adapted to local contexts, actions carried out by other organisations, strategies being pursued, and challenges and opportunities faced. It is a broad concept which encompasses a wide array of elements – legal, budgetary, performance management-related – all of which can have a potentially high importance.

It is rare for management flexibility to be available at all governance levels in the field of employment policy. Our analysis shows that even in countries where decentralisation has led to increasing flexibility at the regional level (for example Belgium, Canada, Italy, Spain), it has yet to filter down to the local level. The area where local level actors appear to have the lowest level flexibility is in the setting of eligibility criteria and performance targets.

However in many respects, the local level has a particularly important role to play in addressing skills and productivity challenges. The level of travel-to-work areas – local labour markets – can be particularly adequate for the task of designing employment and skills development strategies. It is at this level of disaggregation that economic development strategies are often designed. At this level it is also possible to focus on a limited number of industry sectors and clusters within a relatively homogenous economic environment. This can encourage prioritisation and a sharper targeting of programmes. It is also at such a level that employers can determine some common needs, and where labour market authorities locally can have direct contact with employers and economic developers, while keeping track of local social issues and the situation of various vulnerable groups on the labour market.

Due to the increasing importance of partnership working in OECD countries, most local employment agencies now collaborate with, and sit on partnership bodies with other actors to tackle such issues. In nearly all countries, sub-regional offices collaborate with other local actors in this way. In the absence of local decision making power, however, collaboration may in some cases just represent an effort by local public employment service (PES) offices to promote active labour market programmes and targets, rather than to actively work together on the development of new local approaches and strategies.

As this book shows, providing flexibility at the local level does not necessarily require extensive institutional reform. Flexibility can be found in many different institutional contexts. Both small and large countries, unitary or federal countries, show high level of local flexibility, suggesting that there is no correlation between flexibility at local level and the size of the country or the structure of the state. Injecting local flexibility is an equally realistic option in most political and institutional contexts.

Amongst OECD countries, flexibility to co-ordinate and adapt policies locally is currently greatest in Denmark, Switzerland, the United States, Finland and the Czech Republic. While some of these countries have traditionally offered significant autonomies to the local level (for example, Switzerland) changes to the governance structure for employment services over recent years in other countries (particularly Denmark and Finland) have yielded positive results in terms of greater flexibility on the ground.

Despite the fact that the most direct outcomes of such reforms are in the form of processes – the ability to co-ordinate policies and adapt them to local situations using forward-looking strategies, flexibility gained at the local level can be seen to contribute directly to better performance in reducing unemployment and making the labour market more efficient. Econometric analysis presented in this book suggests that sub-regional flexibility is positively and statistically significantly related to employment rates in the countries surveyed. One explanation is that sub-regional flexibility leads to more strategic, responsive and customised active labour market programmes, which in turn direct more training resources to those who need it, resulting in a positive effect on employment rates.

Flexibility is not the only factor important to bringing about change at the local level: capacities, intelligence, and local governance mechanisms are complementary factors that can play a powerful role in helping localities, and countries, to successfully address the opportunities and challenges which arise from today's economic context.

Injecting flexibility also brings its own share of challenges such as how to provide more autonomy while preserving full accountability, and how to make sure that greater flexibility translates into better co-ordination between workforce and economic development. How can the various policy tools and instruments be efficiently organised together in a way that facilitates efficient decision-making on employment and skills development locally?

This publication highlights examples of countries, areas and localities which have tackled these challenges successfully. These examples demonstrate the benefits of integrating skills and employment decisions locally and the need to implement various policy strands on the basis of a common strategy which is forward-looking. It is clear that employment and training organisations today have a great deal of promise for shaping economic development, particularly at the local level, where new economic opportunities and threats are most clearly felt. It is government responsibility to unleash their potential.

ISBN 978-92-64-05918-4
Flexible Policy for More and Better Jobs
© OECD 2009

Chapter 1

A New Framework for Labour Market Policy in a Global Economy

by

Sylvain Giguère and Francesca Froy

Labour market policy is playing an ever important role in helping local economies to return to prosperity and build living standards in a global knowledge based economy. It is increasingly vital to help individuals to fulfil their potential in the labour market and to acquire the skills they need at various stages of their lifetime and in function of new economic opportunities that present themselves. And the demand for skills will need to be enhanced by helping enterprises to raise their productivity. These complex tasks require intensive action at the local level, in partnership with increasingly mobile enterprises and workers. On the ground, a range of government policies need to be co-ordinated and adapted to local conditions – above all, governments need to inject flexibility in the management of policies.

Managing the labour market efficiently is crucial to lifting prosperity and living standards in a global economy, particularly in the aftermath of the recent economic slowdown. It is more vital than ever to help individuals to fulfil their potential in the labour market and to acquire the skills they need at various stages of their lifetime and in function of new economic opportunities that present themselves. And the demand for skills will need to be enhanced by helping enterprises to raise their productivity.

These complex tasks require intensive action at the local level. A range of government policies need to be co-ordinated, adapted to local conditions, and aligned to produce comprehensive and forward-looking strategies. Local staff need to be equipped with the right instruments, intelligence, capacity and strategic autonomy in order to make a difference. Above all, governments need to inject flexibility in the management of policies, to allow local officials enough lee-way to solve local problems and capitalise on local opportunities as they arise.

The governance aspects of employment policies have been the subject of political debates for decades. In many countries there have been calls for decentralisation and devolution. As this book will show, these debates have sometimes been misleading. What is important is not so much whether central or regional government is in charge of employment policy, but the degree of flexibility which is available at the local level to orient programmes in a way that addresses contemporary economic challenges. Significant powers may well need to be exerted by all levels in order to accomplish this mission well. Ministers and high level officials agreed to this principle at a high level conference organised by the OECD in Venice 17-19 April 2009, where they endorsed the Venice Action Statement included as Annex A in this publication.

New complexity arising in the management of labour markets

More than ever, skills determine the destiny of people and places. People with the right skills in the right location can more quickly re-enter the labour market following employment shocks, progress in employment and increase their living standards even while the average wage falls or stagnates in their country. Localities with a skills base that meets the changing job requirements of a high value added sector can enjoy greater economic development, stronger innovative capacities and more positive social outcomes. The sum of these developments in many different localities lifts the competitiveness of the economy as a whole.

FLEXIBLE POLICY FOR MORE AND BETTER JOBS – ISBN 978-92-64-05918-4 – © OECD 2009

Conversely, missed opportunities may have serious implications. After economic shocks, people who have been made redundant find it difficult to quickly obtain new work and can sink into long-term unemployment. Workers see their skills becoming obsolete and face the prospect of decreases in salary and working conditions. Young graduates who hold qualifications that are not in demand remain under-employed even when jobs are simultaneously on offer in their area. In some regions and sectors of the economy, firms operate at the low-productivity end of the market and struggle to improve their processes and products, contributing to poor quality employment and undermining the local skills base.

Helping workers to compete on the world market

Managing the labour market properly today, in a way that will contribute significantly to prosperity, requires tackling new priorities: helping workers to compete on the global market, and moving the local region itself along the path towards the high-skills, high productivity equilibrium.

Before the economic slowdown, globalisation had lifted prosperity and living standards for several decades, both in the advanced and the developing world. At the same time, globalisation and faster progress in technology have been conducive to a greater volatility in the demand for labour and for skills within advanced economies. Recent research has shown that the wage elasticity of the demand for labour more than doubled over the period 1980 to 2002, suggesting that demand is more sensitive to changes in relative wages than before (Hijzen and Swaim, 2007). In the event of rising wage costs, companies are more able to either reduce their recruitment (*e.g.* through investment in new technology or other capital) or move elsewhere. In the event of a trade shock in a given sector of the economy, for example when parts of the production process are off-shored, a more elastic labour demand generates greater negative impacts on both wage and employment.

In addition to wider swings in employment and wages, these developments have fuelled greater wage dispersion and inequality. Various studies show that in many advanced economies the median income has stagnated over the past two or three decades, and that the situation of the low-income families has worsened (OECD, 2007). In Canada, according to the latest Census, incomes have stalled for the past 25 years, with the median earnings of full-time Canadian workers increasing to CAD 41 401 in 2005 from 41 348 in 1980, *i.e.* only about CAD 1 a week more in constant dollars. The income gap between rich and poor has also widened during that period. Young people entering the labour market were earning less in 2005 than their parents did a generation before, and immigrant incomes are on the decrease (Statistics Canada, 2008).

On the face of these developments, and the more direct employment outcomes of the recent global economic slowdown, it is becoming a challenging task for employment agencies to provide the right advice and services to individuals in relation to the labour market. Due to competition with low-wage economies, people who change jobs today sometimes have no choice but to accept lower wages or reduced benefits. Workers who maintain their employment may also see their working conditions reduced for similar reasons. To have a job today is no guarantee of increased living standards. For vulnerable workers, being integrated into the labour market may help in the acquisition of work experience, which can lead to better earnings prospects. But this is not always the case, and it may sometimes be more effective to integrate such individuals into the workforce development system (i.e. training and education) instead (OECD, 2008).

However, providing appropriate and timely training is also becoming an increasingly difficult exercise. Trade economists have recently argued that globalisation has entered a new phase, which is characterised by increased competition at a much more disaggregated level than before. Competition is not anymore only between firms and sectors in different countries, but between workers. Progress in technology makes it possible to fragment the production process into an increasing number of tasks, which can be performed separately from the others, and possibly off-shored.

This new "paradigm" of globalisation suggests that the outcomes of globalisation are becoming more difficult to predict: while globalisation seemed previously to threaten only low-skilled workers, this is no longer the case, with ICT jobs being today typically more mobile. With the fragmentation process being part and parcel of the innovation process, it is difficult to predict future change. Therefore policies to encourage education in high-tech sector-skills may be misled. It is increasingly difficult for government to indicate what sector, job profiles and skills should be privileged in the future (Baldwin, 2006; Blinder, 2006; Grossman and Rossi-Hansberg, 2006).

This has implications for employment and training policy. A first obvious implication is that efforts to help workers adjust to market changes, for example through retraining programmes, should be reinforced. However, a second is that up-skilling strategies need to be well targeted in order to have the right effect. Skills upgrading in sectors which are vulnerable to off-shoring may not help workers increase their security in jobs or obtain better wages or working conditions. Instead, a case by case approach adapted to the potential of individual and local opportunities is better advised.

It is vital for employment and training policy to help individuals to fulfil their potential within the labour market in a way that: i) facilitates their progress in employment over their working life; ii) is based on an analysis of their capacity, education, experience; *iii*) makes reference to possible career paths and current developments within local industry sectors and clusters and *iv*) is sensitive to global trends. For certain workers this may mean upgrading their skills. For others it may require reinforcing mobility within their firm, within their firm's cluster or within their region; for some (particularly vulnerable individuals), it may mean concentrating on soft, basic skills, while for others, acquiring further education. As endogenous development policy seeks to help firms and localities to seize opportunities that arise from globalisation drawing on local assets, labour market policy should behave in the same way for individuals.

The path to high-skills equilibrium

A further challenge concerns the demand for labour and skills. Today business needs change rapidly, and the availability of a qualified pool of labour is an important determinant of business location. As capital becomes increasingly mobile, firms are often quick to move to another location in search of the labour force with the right characteristics.

An increasing problem for employment and training organisations is to get accurate and timely information on those needs so as to adapt programmes and services accordingly. National statistics such as the Labour Force Survey have long lag times and are often too aggregated to be helpful. Local employment and training organisations instead rely on employers to retrieve information on unmet and future business needs. Yet employers have difficulty in determining what their future needs will be. In addition, a portion of future needs in any given locality will be from businesses that do not yet exist or currently operate in another region. Forecasting business needs thus requires an assessment of skills gaps in conjunction with a prospective analysis of economic trends and industry developments.

Preparing a broad and forward-looking analysis also contributes to overcoming certain biases in the demand for skills (Figure 1.1). Firms sometimes strive at the low end of the market for their product and manage to generate margins by using low-tech installations and employing low-qualified workers. When a concentration of such firms exists in a given area or region, most vacancies signalled to employment and training organisations thus concern low-skilled categories of workers. This information in turn drives their activities to place job-seekers and organise training activities.

Such a situation may harm the long-term social and economic prospects of an area. When most placement activities concern low-paid jobs, it may be a sign of grim future for the educated workforce, and young people with diplomas may be tempted to leave the region. A region with a low-educated

Figure 1.1. **Local skills differentiation**

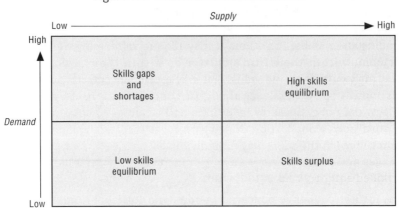

Source: Adapted from Green *et al.* (2003).

workforce will in turn undermine the attractiveness of the local economy for dynamic firms and its capacity to generate new businesses that can thrive well in a knowledge-based economy.

Continuously trying to fulfil needs for low-skill workers can generate moral hazard to the extent that it sends employers signals that they do not need to invest in new technology. They do not need to become more productive as they always get the workers they need. Overall the impact is negative on the competitiveness of the local economy. This situation may also generate social problems if fulfilling short-term needs means resorting to immigration to meet local labour shortages within sectors that are unattractive to local people. If the jobs on offer locally do not ensure satisfactory working and living conditions for locals, they risk doing the same for immigrants. The situation may generate problems of integration for immigrants stuck in low-paid jobs, and high turnover as people do not stay in the region, thereby increasing fixed labour costs (*e.g.* recruitment, job training).

A more efficient local strategy is for public agencies to work with local enterprises to analyse their production process and evaluate how their productivity could be improved. Investment in new technology, introduction of new forms of work organisation, and more management training with the aim of boosting the competitiveness of firms would make it possible for them to hire better qualified people, thereby drawing from the local pool of skilled people. This may make the firms less labour-intensive, however they will generate better-quality jobs which raise prosperity and the skills profile of the local area.

Therefore it is essential for employment and training organisations not only to help improve skills but also to pay attention to the broader mechanisms by which productivity levels can be increased. For this it is necessary to invest simultaneously in the supply and the demand of labour (OECD, 2009b). This will help localities to avoid being trapped in a low-skills equilibrium, where firms thrive at the lower end of the market and offer low-paid jobs (bottom-left corner in Figure 1.1). Joint investment in the supply and demand of skills will help regions move to a high-skills equilibrium, which makes the best use of the talent available locally and stimulates investment in competitive high-performing industry (top-right corner). Investing only in skills supply leads to skills surplus, the flight of talent and high turnover, and is not a stable outcome. Similarly, investing only in the productivity of firms, and not in the supply of skills, will lead to skills shortages and undermine the area's competitiveness until it falls back into a low-skilled equilibrium.

New tasks for new challenges: Decentralisation?

It is therefore simultaneous action on two fronts that today can boost good quality jobs and increase social inclusion: helping individuals to acquire the skills they need at various stages of their lifetime to harness new economic opportunities; and enhancing the demand for skills by encouraging enterprises to raise their productivity levels and become more competitive. This dual strategy requires a new framework for the management of workforce development. The bulk of the work needs to be carried out locally, at a disaggregated level, where opportunities, seized or missed, have huge implications for competitiveness and prosperity. The new policy priorities require intensive work with workers and increasingly mobile enterprises. These tasks thus require a significant degree of autonomy in the conduct of workforce development activities on the ground.

Some of these issues have caused analysts and politicians to press for a greater decentralisation of labour market policy and, in particular, for devolution to regions. Over the past decades, several countries have reformed their public employment service in order to give more autonomy to sub-national levels. Belgium, Canada, Italy, Poland, Spain were among of them. Several other countries more recently embarked in such process, such as the Czech Republic, Denmark, Germany and Korea. A public debate on these issues is still underway in several of these countries and discussions on potential institutional reform of the public employment service have more recently started in others, such as Australia and Japan.

Does decentralisation increase the *effectiveness* of labour market policy? This question has in some ways hampered progress in the debate on decentralisation, as it has been difficult to demonstrate the impact of decentralisation on labour market outcomes. Despite the many studies being released on this topic over recent years, researchers have not been able to identify a solid relationship between decentralisation and policy effectiveness so far.

This is because decentralisation brings both positive and negative impacts, and these impacts offset each other in many instances (Table 1.1) (OECD, 1998). On the positive side, decentralisation brings new and better quality of information into decision making processes thanks to greater proximity with programme participants, target groups and other stakeholders locally. These information gains may translate into smaller deadweight loss (the results of a programme that would have taken place anyway in the absence of that programme) or substitution effect (the results of a programme which reduce outcomes unattended by public policy).

Table 1.1. **Impacts of decentralisation on policy effectiveness**

+	−
Closer to target groups	Duplication of activities
Better information	Uneven capacities
Pragmatic approach	Divergence from main goals

Source: OECD (1998).

On the negative side, if local pilot actions are not mainstreamed, decentralisation can sometimes increase the cost of public policy overall by duplicating within each locality activities that could be more efficiently managed from one central location. Such duplication makes the task of maintaining a satisfactory level of capacity throughout the public infrastructure more difficult.

Another potential negative factor relates, paradoxically, to the pragmatic approach to implementation incentivised by decentralisation. Heralded as a strong advantage of a decentralised system, pragmatism can also mean that local offices take liberties with national policy goals and divert a share of local efforts toward local concerns instead. The most appropriate action to be carried out locally in the light of local conditions and local economic challenges may not be fully compatible with the targets that are imposed by national level actors. For example, targets are often set for the public employment service to increase the employment rate overall. Such a goal may not be appropriate for a region in "low skill equilibrium" where increasing employment by itself would perpetuate the existence of low quality jobs that do not contribute to local prosperity. While undertaking a different set of actions may generate satisfactory outcomes locally, technically, this can undermine the efficiency of the national policy system.

Of course, national policy goals matter. Labour market policy is an important instrument in the macroeconomic policy toolkit. It contributes not only to raising employability but also to other important policy goals, such as keeping inflation low by ensuring that labour markets clear rapidly. Therefore, additional flexibility in its management should in principle not come at the expense of a reduction in overall labour market policy effectiveness.

The experience of a few countries (such as Denmark and the United States) shows that the national policy framework can allow for a greater differentiation in the utilisation of programmes and services locally, while continuing to meet national policy goals. Management by objectives system can allow this, by allowing for targets to be negotiated between the central and the local level, with the national level verifying that the sum of all local targets meets national policy goals. Only a performance management system which ensures full accountability on how policies are implemented can allow for such balanced local/national reconciliation of policy goals, as will be further explored in Chapter 4.

Another difficulty lies in the political context of several countries where administrative regions request more power in the area of workforce development. Decentralisation at a regional level ("regionalisation") can be conducive to more effective policy co-ordination where regional governments already hold responsibilities in economic and social policy. However, labour market authorities in large regions often find themselves as remote from local conditions and industrial challenges as national authorities. They do not have more information than national authorities do in order to more effectively design programmes to meet local needs, and do not benefit from greater proximity to employers or community groups.

More disaggregate levels thus have an important role to play in addressing skills and productivity challenges. The level of travel-to-work areas – local labour markets – can be particularly adequate for the task of designing employment and skills development strategies. It is at this level of disaggregation that economic development strategies are often designed and focused on a limited number of industry sectors and clusters within a relatively homogenous economic environment. This can encourage prioritisation and a sharper targeting of programmes. It is also at such a level that employers can determine some common needs, and where labour market authorities locally can have direct contact with employers and economic developers, while keeping track of local social issues and the situation of various vulnerable groups on the labour market (OECD, 2003; OECD, 2008).

Therefore the process of injecting flexibility should go beyond the political issue of the distribution of powers between the central and regional governments. What is important is that central and regional governments are able to pass on, or share, flexibility with local or sub-regional areas.

Flexibility in OECD countries

So what is the current level of flexibility available to local actors in the management of workforce development policy? The OECD has recently estimated the degree of flexibility available in each country, taking into account the various management aspects of labour market programmes and services: their design, budget, legal framework (including eligibility criteria), performance management, level of outsourcing and collaboration relationships. Estimations have been produced at two governance levels in particular: that of the regional level, and that of the sub-regional/local level (see Chapter 2).

As Figure 1.2 demonstrates, flexibility at local and sub-regional level, where much of the policy co-ordination and adaptation work needs to be carried out, can be found in many different institutional contexts. Both small and large countries, unitary or feral countries, show relatively strong levels of local flexibility, suggesting that there is no correlation between flexibility at local level and the size of the country or the structure of the state. While some federations or countries which reformed their public employment services have recentralised powers at regional level, such as Italy and Belgium, others have managed to pass on key powers to the local level, such as the United States and Austria. Neither does it seem easier to inject flexibility in smaller countries as opposed to large ones. Injecting local flexibility appears an equally realistic option in most political and institutional contexts.

Figure 1.2. **Flexibility in the management of labour market policy**

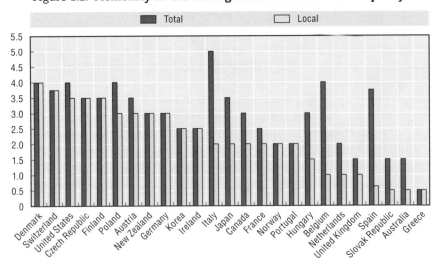

FLEXIBLE POLICY FOR MORE AND BETTER JOBS – ISBN 978-92-64-05918-4 – © OECD 2009

Flexibility in managing labour market policy locally was found to be greatest in Denmark, Switzerland, the United States, Finland and the Czech Republic. The results suggest that reforms of the governance structure for employment services over recent years in some of these countries, such as Denmark and Finland, have yielded positive results in terms of greater flexibility on the ground. Chapter 2 will present these findings in more detail, and analyse the reasons why some countries are doing better than others.

The concept of flexibility in the management of policy has far greater potential than decentralisation with respect to economic analysis. The flexibility indicator built by the OECD refers to the possibility of adjusting labour market policy at its various design, implementation and delivery stages to make it more adapted to local contexts, actions carried out by other organisations, local strategies being pursued, challenges and opportunities faced. It thus approximates the extent to which decisions can be made, notwithstanding the political context – corresponding in fact to "effective" decentralisation. This new indicator allows the recurrent difficulties in analysing the impact from decentralisation to be overcome. Chapter 3 will present the results of quantitative analysis using the indicator which identifies significant correlation with employment outcomes.

Of course, it is not only in the field of labour market policy that local offices can be inflexible. Economic development and vocational training can also have rigidity in the way they operate at local level, which in turn hampers the policy co-ordination process. Overall, flexibility in the management of labour market policy seems to be particularly low compared to other policy areas. Economic development for example is a policy area that enjoys more flexibility. This can be explained by the fact that economic development policies often take the form of financing schemes to support business development projects, which can relatively easily be allocated in accordance with strategies designed regionally or locally. Also, in many countries, economic development policy is designed and implemented regionally, while the national level plays more of an accompanying role (OECD, 2009a, forthcoming).

Partnerships, intelligence and capacity

The potential of flexible local institutions to contribute to the effective implementation of labour market policy at the local level depends on a number of other factors, on which governments also need to focus their attention: partnerships, intelligence and capacity.

Partnerships

There is little that employment agencies can do alone in tackling both the recent economic downturn and the longer term challenges of globalisation.

Local agencies need to capitalise on the flexibility available to them in order to establish meaningful collaborative relationships between employment services, training institutions, economic development organisations, local authorities, employer organisations, trade unions and community-based organisations. In particular strong integration between employment services, economic development agencies and training institutions is necessary to ensure appropriate synergies and trade-offs between different strategic objectives related to human resources development (e.g. integration into employment, skills upgrading, further education, and the attraction of new talent).

Across the OECD over the past two decades partnerships have been set up as a way to foster a joined-approach to problem solving. However, it is important to stress that partnerships can play a meaningful role only if the above recommendations are applied, i.e. there is some flexibility in the management of policy at least at local level. To make local collaboration work, each of the participating organisations needs to have an appropriate level of policy leverage in their field. Unfortunately, this is rarely the case. While partnerships have in many cases proved to be a determinant of positive local outcomes, experience has also shown that their capacity to influence the implementation of policy is very limited. As such the existence of partnerships is not a satisfactory condition for effective policy co-ordination (OECD, 2001; OECD, 2004; OECD, 2005).

Comparisons with other policy fields demonstrate that labour market policy performs poorly in partnerships compared with other policy fields, such as economic development (OECD, 2009a, forthcoming). The officers responsible for economic development at local level are more likely to work in cross-sector partnerships. Their involvement in these partnerships is usually active and transparent as they are more likely to share information and respond to concerns expressed by other stakeholders locally. In comparison, while vocational training and employment service officers participate in numerous partnership initiatives locally, their ability to commit to local strategies is limited by the rigidity they face in the implementation of their programmes and services.

Local data and intelligence

If employment and training organisations are to have a broader and more important role locally, this means that they will require a deeper and broader source of data and intelligence to guide their actions. In particular, it is important for labour market organisations to develop greater knowledge about their local economy. Knowing the answer to the question "What are the current challenges brought by globalisation, environmental change and progress in technology to local industry?" will be a prerequisite in future years to providing the right guidance in terms of enhancing productivity and tackling skills gaps. A second area where intelligence needs to be developed by labour market organisations is in relation to career paths. What are the possible career paths for local workers in each cluster or sector of the local economy given the training infrastructure, the qualifications needed to progress from a job profile to another and the future industrial developments expected? Given that the new paradigm of globalisation casts doubts on the usefulness of some training options, it is increasingly important to be able to foster mobility across job profiles and employers within the same network of enterprises. To make the best of this opportunity for job progression, it is vital to have a strong knowledge of the structure of local clusters and of the skills required by the various job profiles they contain.

In the absence of strong disaggregated information from national sources, new sources of data and intelligence must be built locally. Local surveys must be carried out regularly to identify business needs and skills gaps. Further analysis is usually required to identify and analyse the opportunities and threats facing local industry, and assess the implications for the local skills base and competitiveness of local firms. Having the representation of employer and private sector representatives on local strategic partnerships is a further important way of harnessing knowledge about likely economic trends.

The production of this information locally is a difficult exercise inasmuch as statistical and analytical capacities are often limited. It is often advisable to involve local universities, research centres and consultants, though such participation often comes at a price. Governments have a role to play in providing resources that can be invested in the production of local data and intelligence locally. A range of analytical tools can also be provided at national level to facilitate analysis at local level (see OECD, 2006a; OECD, 2006b). At the same time it is vital that any information gathered is jointly "owned" by a number of different local institutions so that they have a common understanding of local assets, opportunities and threats.

Capacity

The role outlined for employment and training organisations above is a relatively new one, and as such will take a while to be properly understood and absorbed by local institutions. Employment service staff often receive relatively specific training in relation to programme implementation and claim management. They rarely receive guidance on the broader policy framework for labour market policy, and on other policy fields such as economic development and innovation. OECD research shows that employment services and training organisations sometimes thus lack the necessary skills for participating in collective strategic exercises and managing projects involving several sponsors (OECD, 2009a, forthcoming).

Indeed there is a growing body of thought that local actors need specific training in the generic skills necessary for partnership and collaborative working to achieve properly joined up local strategies.[1]

It is essential that governments take action to build the strategic capacity of local staff. Goals must be defined locally, that are compatible with the strengths and weaknesses of the local skills base and industry sectors. This means taking a proactive approach, and an ability to take initiatives that help advance strategic objectives. It also means the capacity to establish strong collaboration with other stakeholders locally, such as business partners and local authorities, and to involve them in the pursuit of shared goals.

Applications

So what would be the outcome of the suggested changes in the management and delivery of labour market policy? What can be done in practice with a reasonable degree of flexibility and capacity, effective local governance mechanisms and an informative intelligence base? Research shows that where the best use is made of the possibilities available locally to produce joined up strategies (OECD, 2009b, forthcoming) this can enable localities to:

- Connect decisions to attract workers, upgrade the skills of the low-qualified and integrate the vulnerable (*e.g.* immigrants) not only into jobs but into the workforce development system. As Chapter 6 will show, these decisions are often fragmented locally, taken by different organisations and on the basis of partial information, leading to inefficient use of public funds and allocation of human resources.

- Tackle skills gaps in enterprises while also addressing productivity issues. Fulfilling the recruitment needs of enterprises needs to be combined with a responsibility for employers to use human resources in the best way possible. Possibilities to help local businesses to invest in new technology to become more competitive and to offer better jobs should be taken up.

- Anticipate change. Cases surveyed confirm that employment and training organisations can play an important role as leaders to foster and anticipate change. They contribute to the design of economic development strategies which embed a strong human resource dimension. They are likely to be more responsive to potential opportunities and threats because of their employment implications, and hence focused on a limited number of priorities.

Michigan provides a good example of how the new priorities for labour market policies can be addressed in practice (see OECD, 2009b). In 2004, the Governor of Michigan embarked on a state-wide project to improve the efficiency of local workforce development and educational systems in meeting businesses needs. For many years, Michigan has invested in an extensive and renowned post-secondary educational system, and in partnership with the federal government it has developed a comprehensive workforce system. However, there has been increasing concern that these two systems are not collaborating sufficiently to meet the needs of Michigan's business community. Recognising that local labour markets have their own specific needs and that local entities best understand them, the state turned to local stakeholders to form partnerships to identify skills needs, develop the strategies to address the needs, and carry out proposed activities. With the financial assistance of the Charles Stewart Mott Foundation (a charitable foundation located in Michigan), the state offered one-year start-up grants totalling over USD 1 million for the initial development of 13 "regional skills alliances" (MiRSAs) across the state. Nine of these skills alliances were convened by workforce boards; the other four were convened by a labour organisation, two post-secondary training programmes, and a community-based organisation. The overall goal was to provide employers with a highly skilled labour force but also to provide local citizens, particularly lower income individuals, with jobs that offer good wages and promising opportunities for career advancement.

The regional skills alliances, set up at a sub-regional level, were asked to focus on a very limited number of industry sectors, which contributed to sharpening economic development strategies. In each sector they connected the human resources-related decisions with a view to invest both in the supply and the demand for skills. Figure 1.3 outlines the case of the sector of

Figure 1.3. **Healthcare regional skills alliance of Northwest Michigan**

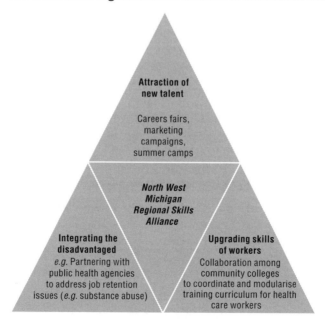

health care in the area of North West Michigan. The health care sector faces labour shortages in this area of Michigan amongst others. Taking an integrated approach to employment and skills development has allowed the region to fill skill gaps while also paying attention to improving the career opportunities available within healthcare through formalising career ladders, and working with local colleges on courses to up-skill current employees as they progress through the system.

This example, like many others at the local level within OECD countries, demonstrates the importance of integrating skills and employment decisions locally and the need to implement the various policy strands on the basis of a common strategy which is forward-looking. It means that the work of employment agencies should be much more proactive and intelligence-based (in terms of career paths and the current challenges from globalisation to the local industry). Some degree of flexibility in the management of labour market policy is needed for workforce development to be suitably co-ordinated with economic development and adapted to local conditions.

Conclusion

The challenges brought by globalisation and technological progress, exacerbated by the global economic crisis, translate into new tasks for labour market institutions. Far from undermining the role of employment and training organisations, globalisation calls on the contrary for more intelligence gathering, more partnership building, and more strategic thinking. Such activism does not always fit with the standardised procedures of employment and training organisations. This is why changes are required on multiple fronts, from adapting the policy management framework to building capacities on the ground.[2]

In this field, it is practice that shows the way, not theory. In a number of OECD countries, local employment agencies, training institutions and economic development organisations are taking initiatives in the direction described in this chapter, taking advantage of, or acting in spite of their governance systems and policy frameworks. A number of different actions have been carried out in this context by employment and training organisations, and this book will uncover some of them.

To trigger such initiatives, sometimes only a change in perspective suffices. Some employment services see themselves as insufficiently-funded public agencies constrained by their performance management framework. Taking a drastically different vantage point, other organisations, operating under similar constraints, view the set of targets they have to reach by year end only as a starting point, planning more ambitious activities with other local actors. The most confident local organisations will conclude successful partnerships with the private sector and non-government organisations, launch intelligence-building processes, raise further resources and bring more expertise on board.

Employment and training organisations have a great deal of promise for shaping the impact of globalisation at the local level. And indeed, much of this work can only be done locally, where opportunities and threats are most clearly felt. It is government responsibility to unleash the potential in this regard. By doing so, they will better be able to tackle more immediate labour market shocks and support local economic growth whilst also reaching their national goals of prosperity, social inclusion and competitiveness.

Notes

1. See, for example, the United Kingdom's Academy for Sustainable Communities: *www.ascskills.org.uk/pages/home.*

2. These recommendations were adopted by labour ministers at the High-Level Conference on Decentralisation and Co-ordination: The Twin Challenges of Labour Market Policy, held in Venice on 17-19 April 2008 (see Venice Action Statement in Annex A), and endorsed by the OECD LEED Directing Committee (9-10 June 2008). They are based on the analysis of the experience of OECD countries by the LEED Programme throughout a series of projects conducted within the framework of its work agenda on employment and governance over the past decade (*More than Just Jobs*, 2008; *From Immigration to Integration*, 2006b; *Skills Upgrading*, 2006a; *Local Governance and the Drivers of Growth*, 2005; *New Forms of Governance for Economic Development*, 2004; *Managing Decentralisation*, 2003; *Local Partnerships for More Effective Governance*, 2001).

Bibliography

Baldwin, R. (2006), "Globalisation: The Great Unbundling(s)", Report prepared for the Economic Council of Finland as part of Finland's EU Presidency programme, September.

Blinder, A.S. (2006), "Offshoring: The Next Industrial Revolution?", *Foreign Affairs*, 85:2, 113-128.

Green, A.E, C. Hasluck, T. Hogarth and C. Reynolds (2003), "East Midlands FRESA Targets Project – Final Report", *Report for East Midlands Development Agency*, Institute for Employment Research, University of Warwick, and Pera.

Grossman, G. and E. Rossi-Hansberg (2006), "The Rise of Offshoring: It's Not Wine for Cloth Anymore", *Proceedings*, Federal Reserve Bank of Kansas City, Kansas City, pp. 59-102.

Hijzen, A. and P. Swaim (2007), "Offshoring, Labour Market Institutions and the Elasticity of Labour Demand", *GEP Research Paper 08/05*, The Leverhulme Centre for Research on Globalisation and Economic Policy, University of Nottingham, UK.

OECD (1998), *Local Management for More Effective Employment Policy*, OECD Publishing, Paris.

OECD (2001), *Local Partnerships for Better Governance*, OECD Publishing, Paris.

OECD (2003), *Managing Decentralisation: A New Role for Labour Market Policy*, OECD Publishing, Paris.

OECD (2004), *New Forms of Governance for Economic Development*, OECD Publishing, Paris.

OECD (2005), *Local Governance and the Drivers of Growth*, OECD Publishing, Paris.

OECD (2006a), *Skills Upgrading: New Policy Perspectives*, OECD Publishing, Paris.

OECD (2006b), *From Immigration to Integration: Local Solutions to a Global Challenge*, OECD Publishing, Paris.

OECD (2007), "OECD Workers in the Global Economy: Increasingly Vulnerable?", *Employment Outlook*, Chapter 3, OECD Publishing, Paris.

OECD (2008), *More than Just Jobs: Workforce Development in a Skills-based Economy*, OECD Publishing, Paris.

OECD (2009a, forthcoming), *Breaking Out of Silos: Joining Up Policy Locally*, OECD Publishing, Paris.

OECD (2009b, forthcoming), *Designing Local Skills Strategies*, OECD Publishing, Paris.

Statistics Canada (2008), *Census 2006*, Government of Canada, Ottawa.

ISBN 978-92-64-05918-4
Flexible Policy for More and Better Jobs
© OECD 2009

Chapter 2

Which Countries Have Most Flexibility in the Management of Labour Market Policy? An OECD Comparison

by
Francesca Froy and Sylvain Giguère

In order for labour market policy to contribute fully to competitiveness, inclusion and prosperity at the local level, flexibility is necessary in the management of policies and programmes. This chapter presents the results from research conducted in 25 OECD countries to evaluate the degree of flexibility available in the management of labour market policies and programmes at both the regional and local levels. Denmark, Switzerland, the United States, Finland and the Czech Republic present the highest degree of flexibility at the level of local labour markets (or "travel to work" areas), followed by Austria, New Zealand and Poland. In general, however, there is some way to go before offices at this level have an adequate level of flexibility to fully adapt employment policy to local needs and to priorities set in partnership with other local actors.

Flexibility in the management of labour market policies and programmes is central to optimising the contribution of local employment agencies to competitiveness, inclusion and prosperity at the local level. OECD research shows that flexibility is not necessarily correlated with particular forms of labour market decentralisation or devolution, but can be present in any public employment system. Indeed, it cannot be ruled out that a given centralised system provides more flexibility than a decentralised or devolved one. The comparison of local flexibility across the OECD outlined below therefore goes beyond an analysis of the types of administrative and political structure existing in each country to examine the sort of management flexibility allowed to labour market agencies working at the local level.

What do we mean by local?

By local, we mean here the level of local labour markets – sometimes known as "travel to work areas",[1] where economic development strategies are frequently designed and where local policy makers have the opportunity of a strong level of contact with local businesses, sectors and clusters in addition to non-governmental organisations and community groups. This does not necessarily correspond to the municipal level, where the public employment service has its antennas. Such municipal offices are often merely delivery agencies with low critical mass and strategic capacity, except in urban centres.

In order to reflect this territorial subtlety, we distinguish in our analysis between three levels of government and/or administration, when the size of the country permits:

1. **Regional level:** administrative regions with a population of between 800 000 and 3 million (NUTS 2, following the nomenclature used by the European Union).

2. **Sub-regional level:** smaller regions with a population of between 150 000 and 800 000 (the equivalent of NUTS 3).

3. **Local level or municipal level:** localities under 150 000 (the equivalent of NUTS 4).

The **sub-regional level** corresponds to areas of less than 800 000 inhabitants, and therefore offices operating at this level and below are considered to be working at the level of local labour markets for the purposes of this analysis. To build up a picture of the flexibility available for labour market agencies at this,

FLEXIBLE POLICY FOR MORE AND BETTER JOBS – ISBN 978-92-64-05918-4 – © OECD 2009

and other administrative levels, questions have been posed to national ministries on different aspects of the management of labour market policies and programmes.[2]

What aspects of flexibility are we looking at?

Labour ministries in OECD countries hold their offices[3] responsible for delivering their employment policy accountable in various different ways, either through controlling the programmes which are delivered, the use of budgets, the eligibility criteria for who should receive training and support, the types of staff (internal or outsourced) who deliver programmes and the setting of performance targets. Box 2.1 lists the aspects which can have an influence on the flexibility available to actors and agencies at each administrative level. In more traditional systems of public administration, the accountability framework emphasises legal and fiscal accountability and the separation of administration and politics, whereas "new public management"

Box 2.1. **What do we mean by flexibility?**

Programme design: Do sub-regional offices have any input into the design of policies and programmes? Are they consulted? Are they free to determine the programme mix and even adapt design features of programmes, including target groups, or are these largely centrally determined? May local Public Employment Service (PES) offices implement innovative programmes outside the standard programme portfolio? Do they design local employment strategies?

Financing: Do sub-regional actors have flexible global budgets or line item budgets for active measures? Are they free to allocate resources flexibly between budget items for active measures?

Target groups: Are local offices free to decide on the target groups for their assistance locally or do programmes already specify particular target groups?

Goals and performance management: To what extent are organisational goals and targets centrally determined? Do they allow room for sub-regional goals and hence flexibility in adapting goals to local circumstances? Are targets and indicators hierarchically imposed or negotiated with regional and local actors? Is performance assessment based solely on quantitative criteria? Are sanctions imposed if targets are not met?

Collaboration: Are local offices free to participate in partnerships and do they collaborate with other actors? Can local offices decide who they collaborate with locally?

Outsourcing: Are local offices responsible for outsourcing services to external providers?

---

gives greater emphasis to decentralisation, managerial discretion, performance measures, quality standards and client satisfaction in accountability frameworks. In each case, local actors can have greater or lesser freedom to implement policy as they see fit to meet local needs, and to contribute effectively to local strategies.

For the purposes of this research, we have looked at the degree of flexibility available to local agencies in six main areas:

1. designing programmes;

2. allocating budgets;

3. defining target groups;

4. setting performance criteria;

5. collaborating with other actors; and

6. outsourcing.

We have scored countries against the degree of flexibility available and used the results of our research to allocate an overall index of local flexibility between 0 and 5 for each country, which has been used to perform an initial international comparison.[4]

The product of decentralisation: Flexibility at the regional level but not at the local level?

In order to compare flexibility at the different governance levels, we have looked first at the total level of flexibility available below the national level (a total for regional, sub-regional and local), and secondly more specifically at the flexibility available at the sub-regional level and below. Figure 2.1 provides estimates of the total degree of flexibility available to policy makers in the implementation of labour market policy at all administrative levels beneath that of the national government. The results indicate particularly high sub-national flexibility in countries which have devolved power down to the regional level through wide-ranging reforms (Italy, Belgium, Poland, Spain) and countries which are federated states (Austria, Switzerland and the United States). The Czech Republic, Denmark, Finland, and Japan also show significant degrees of overall decentralisation.

However, this ranking differs significantly when it comes to looking at the flexibility available to labour market agencies working at the local and sub-regional levels, i.e. the level of local labour markets. Many of those countries which have strong devolved regions offer a significantly lower degree of flexibility to their labour market agencies working at local/sub-regional level, and most notably in Belgium, Italy and Spain (Figure 2.2).

Figure 2.1. **Sum of flexibility available to agencies and departments operating below the national level**

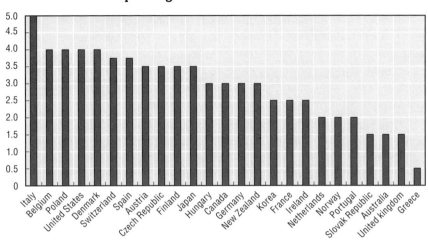

Figure 2.2. **Flexibility available to agencies and departments operating at the sub-regional level**

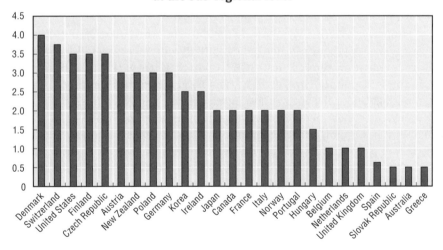

Countries showing the highest level of local flexibility

When it comes to flexibility at the sub-regional level, the analysis reveals that Denmark, Switzerland, the United States, Finland and the Czech Republic present the highest degree of flexibility. The sections below detail how they achieved this. At the other end of the spectrum, Australia, Belgium, Greece, Netherlands, Spain, the Slovak Republic and the United Kingdom appear to offer relatively little flexibility to local level offices when it comes to implementing labour market policy.

Within this group, Greece, the Slovak Republic and the United Kingdom operate a centralised Public Employment Service (PES) system which retains the majority of flexibility at the national level. This is changing in the case of the United Kingdom, however, which in 2008 introduced a "flexible new deal" which will offer local public employment service officials more choice in how they help longer term unemployed people into work.

Australia is somewhat of a special case as it has principally outsourced its services to the private sector, which it manages from the central level with some help from the states.[5] In the Netherlands, labour market policy is also mainly sub-contracted out to private, public and non-profit providers. Dutch municipalities are responsible for the implementation of subsistence benefit and in this case the system is particularly decentralised, but this is not taken into account by the present analysis, which focuses on active labour market programmes and employment services targeting those people receiving unemployment benefits. For the shorter term unemployed receiving unemployment benefits, services are delivered by the UWV (*Uitvoeringsinstituut WerknemersVerzekeringen*) where flexibility is only available at the regional levels.

Similarly, in Germany, following the Hartz reforms, there are two separate laws governing labour market policy: SGB III which is targeted towards the short term unemployed and SGB II, which is targeted towards longer unemployed people (in Germany, insurance benefits usually last only 12 months). Under the second law, municipalities and PES offices (which have in many cases now been brought together) have been given a high level of flexibility in administering programmes. This includes being able to choose the mix of programmes that are delivered at the local level to meet the needs of their target group and having full discretion on the use of budgets within the limits of the goals for national policy delivery. However, this applies only to persons receiving means-tested benefits and is therefore not included in the analysis.

Flexibility by management tools

Below we compare results for OECD countries for each aspect of the management of labour market policy initially summarising the results and then providing more details on the countries studied.

Design of labour market programmes

Overall, local actors do not seem to have a significant role in the design of labour market policies and programmes in OECD countries. As outlined below, local actors only actively design active labour market programmes in just over a quarter of all the countries studied (28%). A similar proportion of local offices (24%) do not design programmes, but can choose the mix of programming delivered locally, while in one in five countries, local offices are consulted when programmes are being developed. Over a quarter also actively develop local employment *strategies* as opposed to programmes. In just under a third of countries (32%) local actors have no role at all in designing active labour market programmes (see Table 2.1).

Inputting into the design of programmes

The most freedom to influence labour market programmes and policies can be found in Switzerland, Denmark, Finland and Poland. In Switzerland, for example, the legal basis for the use of labour market policy measures is defined at federal level, however, the cantons decide on measures tailor-made for local needs. Nearly all the cantons have created measures to support job seekers (training and employment measures). Cantons often also promulgate special laws in relation to implementation. In Denmark, local job centres can choose from a set of different activities (counselling, training, wage subsidies and specific job referrals) to design programmes for those that they identify as being most in need of support while paying attention to national priorities. In Finland, the sub-regional T&E offices as well as the local PES offices draft active labour market programmes in consultation with social partners and other local actors. In Poland, general labour market policy guidelines are defined on the national level, but local *poviat* labour offices have the possibility to complement them while developing labour market programmes in line with local labour market needs.

In several cases, local offices design labour market programmes that are additional to those developed at the national level. In the Slovak Republic, the district offices of Labour, Social Affairs and Family (LSAF) are involved in designing special projects and programmes to improve the employment situation in their relevant territorial district, both alone and in partnership. In the United States, the programme managers in local one-stop centres may design employment interventions, consistent with applicable federal and state laws and the polices of state and local workforce investment boards (WIBs), to meet the needs of local job seekers and employers. In Korea, a new system was introduced in 2006 where local job centres can also design additional employment service programmes and vocational/career guidance programmes to reflect local characteristics. The headquarters of the Ministry of Labour review such programmes and based on the results of its review, financially support the costs.

Some countries allow selected local areas to have more of an input into the design of labour market policy, either as part of a pilot, or because they are

Table 2.1. **Flexibility available at the local and sub-regional levels**

	Programme design					Budgets				Eligibility			Performance management				Outsourcing	Collaboration
	No flexibility	Are consulted	Design strategies	Can choose mix	Involved in design	No flexibility	Special funding	Can move funding	Block grant	No flexibility	Some freedom to decide	Set criteria	N/A	No flexibility	Negotiate targets	Set targets	Involved at local level	Involved in partnerships
Australia	●					●				●				●				●
Austria				●		●	●	●	●					●				●
Belgium	●		●	●						●							●	●
Canada[1]										●								●
Czech Republic			●	●	●		●		●			●			●		●	●
Denmark			●		●		●	●			●			●			●	●
Finland			●					●							●			●
France			●					●			●				●		●	●
Germany				●	●[2]						●				●			●
Greece	●									●			●					●
Hungary		●		●			●				●						●	●
Ireland		●	●			●				●				●				●
Italy						●		●		●	●			●	●[3]			●
Japan		●	●			●	●				●							●
Korea					●[2]					●					●		●	●
Netherlands		●		●						●	●			●			●	●
New Zealand		●								●				●			●	●
Norway				●				●		●				●			●	●
Poland									●	●					●		●	●
Portugal	●				●[2]			●		●			●					●
Slovak Republic	●					●				●			●				●	●
Spain					●	●				●				●				●
Switzerland									●	●							●	●
United Kingdom	●	●								●				●				●
United States					●[2]			●			●				●[3]		●	●

1. Results for co-managed provinces only.
2. In addition to delivering national programmes.
3. Local offices also set additional targets for their own offices.

areas with special needs. In Japan, for example, local authorities in assisted areas design employment programmes for approval by the Minister of Health, Labour and Welfare, and after this the government provides the required assistance.

Influencing the mix of programming

A further set of countries allow their local offices to have some influence on the mix of programmes delivered locally. In Austria, it is up to the regional and finally local offices, to decide which national programmes they use. For example, the national goal "prevention of long-term unemployment" may be achieved by national programmes to support effective job matching or training, by an employment programme or by outsourced activities. The local PES offices have the flexibility to decide how to prioritise programmes locally. In Belgium, the communes in Brussels can choose the composition of their labour market activities according to local needs although this flexibility is not available in the region of Flanders. In the Czech Republic, the Employment Service Administration develops annual ALMP programmes for individual district labour offices (DLOs) based on an analysis of local labour markets and in compliance with objectives set at national level. However, in reality DLOs are entitled to diverge from the determined programmes, as long as this is justified, and are largely independent in determining what tools they use.

In France, local deconcentrated PES offices have the liberty to choose between national programmes to produce a "tool box" which is adapted as possible to their locality. In the Netherlands, within the central labour market policy framework, local Centre for Work and Income offices may find room for local tailor-made arrangements with municipalities and the UWV (which delivers active labour market policy for those on employment insurance). In Norway, in principle, local offices are also encouraged to decide what measures are most appropriate to get good results.

Consulted

In addition, local level offices are in some cases consulted on the development of national policies. The prefectural labour bureaus and local public employment security offices are consulted when basic regional policies are being formulated at national level in Japan. In Hungary, the service centres and branch offices do not have eligibility to decide on which active labour market programmes to deliver, however they are sometimes involved in the planning of these programmes. In New Zealand, a Regional Social Policy Group was established in 2004, which has resulted in regional policy advisors being placed in regional Ministry for Social Development offices (at sub-regional level). A key role of these policy advisors is to identify issues of importance to the regions and have these considered by national policy makers, as well as providing regional information about how well policies are working on the ground. Regional offices are also involved in the development of policy as part of an internal consultation process. In the United States, state and local areas are also consulted on the development of federal programmes, generally through the federal legislative process, and/or through the federal regulatory process.

Strategic design

While local PES offices are not always responsible for developing or designing active labour market programmes, they are often nevertheless involved in designing local employment based strategies. For example, in France, the objective of the local "*Maisons de l'emploi*" is to integrate policies around a common local strategy based on an analysis, plan of action and set of programmes. In Belgium, the sub-regional employment committees have an important role in the development of local employment strategies and co-ordinating labour market policy. In Ireland, the directors of regional offices are responsible for regional strategies in order to ensure that the needs of the local labour market are met.

Budgets

Countries also vary in the degree to which local level Public Employment Service offices have autonomy and flexibility in the management of budgets (again see Table 2.1). In just under a third of cases (32%), local PES offices have no freedom in the use of their budgets. However 16% of offices receive "block grants" which they can use to fund active labour market programmes as they saw fit. In 40% of countries local actors can move funding between budget lines to better adapt interventions to local circumstances. In just under a quarter of countries (24%), local actors are given special funds to support innovative approaches adapted to local needs.

Block grants and/or can choose which programmes to fund

As noted above, in some OECD countries, local offices receive block grants to spend on active labour market policy. For example, in Denmark, local job centres receive a financial envelope that they can spend how they wish (although they receive separate funding streams for active labour market policy and staffing or administrative costs). In addition, a potentially limitless amount of reimbursement is available for wage subsidies. In Switzerland, the cantons also receive a block grant to organise employment and training activation measures based on the average number of registered job seekers per year. In Poland, the employment offices at *voivodship* level allocate an envelope of labour fund resources received from the central level to the *poviat* level according to a given algorithm. In Austria, the local PES offices can spend their budget as they wish on different programmes and instruments in order to achieve required goals and objectives.

Moving funding between budget lines

It is more common, however, for local PES offices to receive line budgets but have some freedom to move funding where needed between budget lines. In Germany, for example, line budgets for active measures under SGB III for short term unemployed people have been merged into a single "reintegration budget" with local offices being free to determine the mixture of measures implemented, while still being obliged to offer all types of measure. In Finland, the sub-regional T&E centres negotiate a yearly budget for active labour market measures and can reallocate this if needed (*e.g.* more funding to labour market training and less to subsidised work). The local PES offices in Finland also have a possibility to suggest reallocation of funds, with reallocations being reported to the national ministry several times a year. In Norway, the local offices also have some possibility to shift funds between measures, while the local level in larger cities (in some cases larger than most counties) may have more autonomous resources allocated.

In Portugal, transfers of appropriations are permitted from one local job centre budget to another providing certain conditions are met. In the United Kingdom, the local PES offices have autonomy to move money within staffing budget lines, and also within non-staffing budget lines. In Ireland, regional offices of the FÁS determine how budgets are spent at a local/regional level and can request that the national level shifts funds between budget lines. In Italy, the provincial level also has some freedom to shift funding between budget lines. In France, since 1998 there has been more freedom for deconcentrated Public Employment Service offices (at the level of the department) to transfer funds between programmes to better adapt their toolkit of services to local needs. This liberty is available for roughly 30% of the budget. In Canada, local PES offices are more restricted in that they are only able to move money within programmes (*e.g.* due to over subscription or lack of relevance of certain programme strands) and not between programmes (*e.g.* from Youth programmes to Older Worker programmes, for example).

Funding to support innovative measures

In a number of countries, local PES offices are allocated special funds to support measures that are adapted to local and regional needs. In Germany, for example, 10% of funding to support the shorter term unemployed (SGB III) can be spent on innovative measures at the local level. In Austria, again about 10% of the labour market budget can be used freely to meet regional/local needs. In Denmark, local offices can receive additional funds (equating to roughly 10% of their budget) for developing initiatives to meet regional "bottleneck" areas in the labour market, which are identified and reviewed every 6 months at the level of the employment regions. In the Czech Republic, district labour offices may also apply for extra funding for regional targeted employment programmes aimed at addressing employment growth at the local and sub-regional levels. In New Zealand, the Regional Commissioners for Social Development have discretionary funds of approximately 15% of their budget to support innovative local employment related projects. They are offered a choice of innovative programmes (e.g. to support enterprising communities, local industry partnerships, skill investment, work experience, self employment and outcomes based contracting) and can decide on the split dependant on the local labour markets and the outcomes required. In Korea, as noted above, job centres design employment service programmes to reflect local characteristics and these are reviewed and if successful funded by the Ministry of Labour.

In the cases of Australia, Belgium, Greece, Hungary, Japan, Netherlands, Spain and the Slovak Republic there appeared to be little flexibility in the management of budgets at the local level. It should be remembered however, that in many cases local actors had other funds which they could use to support innovative employment activities, such as the European Structural Funds. In some cases, Public Employment Service funds are also complemented by local and regional funds, e.g. from the municipal tax base. In these cases, local actors evidently have much greater flexibility and freedom in developing and using budgets.

Eligibility criteria

Decisions on eligibility and allocation of services to specific target groups appear to be taken for the most part at the national level, with local actors having little freedom in this area in over half of all countries. In only one country (the Czech Republic), local actors are free to set their own eligibility criteria, while in 40% of cases they have some freedom in providing services to individuals within broad national guidelines.

In the Czech Republic, the district labour offices (DLOs) are quite independent in terms of setting eligibility criteria for the participation in ALMP programmes. According to their local needs, the DLOs decide on the tools to be used, on the most problematic groups to be targeted and on the amounts of money to be spent on each tool and group. Each DLO has developed an internal norm which is followed when selecting jobseekers to programmes.

Elsewhere, some discretion is provided to local PES offices within national guidelines. In Denmark, while the national level identifies three main target areas – youth, the long term unemployed (over 3 months) and the sick – within this local offices can decide which groups they particularly want to focus on (*e.g.* women, ethnic minorities, immigrants, the low or high skilled). In Austria, the national level also considers that there is considerable room for manoeuvre by local PES offices in deciding who to support on the basis of identified need in the field of active labour market policy. In Germany, under SGB III for short term unemployed people the choice of target groups for participation of jobseekers in employment and training measures is determined by the placing staff in the local employment agencies for discretionary measures. In Japan, discretion is given to prefectural labour bureaus and local public employment security offices in selecting target groups for certain measures. In New Zealand, eligibility criteria are also set at the national level, however a new service approach allows regional offices to tailor their services to an individual's circumstances and work-readiness, instead of making decisions based on their benefit type.

Performance targets

Similarly, in terms of performance management, local offices have a low level of freedom to set their own performance targets. However they are able to negotiate these targets set by national and regional levels and/or set additional targets for their own offices in just over half of all cases (48%).

Local labour offices negotiate targets with regional and national offices in Austria, Canada, Czech Republic, Denmark, Finland, Germany, Ireland, Japan, Korea, New Zealand, Portugal and the United States. For example, in the United States, the Workforce Investment Act focuses on three performance measures: entered employment, retention, and earnings levels. All local and state workforce boards are held accountable for achieving minimum thresholds for each measure. The thresholds are negotiated first between the federal government and the states; and then the states, once their thresholds have been established, negotiate with their local workforce boards in order to meet their state thresholds. Performance measures are published quarterly, and failure to meet these thresholds may result in funds being withheld. In Denmark, the local job centres produce annual reports which are used by the employment regions as a basis for advising the national level on appropriate outcome targets in relation to the three priority areas of the long-term unemployed, the sick and youth. These then feed back down into locally agreed targets.

In some countries the local offices also set additional targets to those set at higher governance levels. For example, in Japan, in fiscal year 2007, nationwide targets were set by prefectural labour bureaus and local PES offices for two indicators: the "employment rate" of job applicants and the "early reemployment rate" of people eligible for employment insurance benefit and these local targets were combined to form national targets. In addition to these national targets, ten operational targets are set nationwide such as employment numbers for people with disabilities, while the prefectural labour bureaus and local PES offices also set additional targets suited to the situation of each locality and region. In Korea, within the new decentralised delivery structure local and regional PES offices (*Shi*, *Gun* and *Gu* levels) autonomously establish annual plans for key projects to be undertaken in consultation with the national level and in doing so, voluntarily set performance targets. At the end of the year they use these performance indicators to assess whether target have been reached and those offices which achieve the highest score are awarded.

Collaboration with other local actors

In almost all countries, local PES offices work in partnership with other actors. The type of actors they work with include large enterprises, schools, trade unions and business representatives, city development boards, organisations to support entrepreneurship, local skills bodies and colleges, primary health organisations, career counselling agencies, temporary work agencies, and non-government organisations (NGOs). In some cases this is formalised. For example, in Belgium, sub-regional committees have been set up (the RESOC and SERRs in Flanders, CSEF and MIRE in Wallonia, and BNCTO in Brussels) which are broad platforms to discuss employment policy including employers, local authorities, educational actors and others. In Flanders the regional level (VDAB) has established co-operation accords with a number of different regional actors (for example the third sector, sectoral groups, associations of communes and towns) and must approve partnerships developed at lower governance levels. In Finland the T&E centres operate under tri-partite boards, which explains the strong involvement of social partners in programme design at the local level. In Denmark, local job centres are also free to decide on the makeup of local "employment councils" that oversee their work, although they need to include at least the social partners, municipalities and organisations dealing with invalidity issues, and to respect a tri-partite balance. In France, since 1998 the type of collaboration which local offices may engage with has been controlled more tightly by the state in order to consolidate actions and prevent duplication. In other cases, local agencies are given more freedom to collaborate as they see fit.

Outsourcing

Finally, local offices are relatively likely to be involved in outsourcing active labour market services. In roughly two thirds of countries (64%) local offices are involved in outsourcing, with larger regions taking this responsibility in just under a quarter of countries (Table 2.1). The type of

FLEXIBLE POLICY FOR MORE AND BETTER JOBS – ISBN 978-92-64-05918-4 – © OECD 2009

activities to be outsourced include specialist activities to support people in their job search (*e.g.* job clubs) and the targeting of particular groups. In most cases a mix of public and private providers are used, with non-government organisations often being felt to be best placed to work with disadvantaged groups in the labour market for example.

In many cases, however, local and regional offices follow national guidelines and templates when outsourcing. In Australia, for example, while both regional and national bodies are responsible for contracting out to providers, the survival of a provider depends on its "star-rating" which emerges from a national quasi-econometric statistical exercise which takes into account variables representing local circumstances (unemployment rate, etc.) but does not allow regions any freedom to give more weight to particular target groups.

Comparison between different aspects of the management of policies and programmes

Overall local PES offices have the highest level of flexibility in the area of collaboration with other actors (Figure 2.3). In all cases, with the exception of Japan, the sub-regional offices collaborated with other local actors in partnership. In the absence of local decision making power, however, collaboration may in some cases represent an effort by local PES offices to promote active labour market programmes and targets, rather than to actively work together on the development of new local approaches and strategies.

Figure 2.3. **Comparison between flexibility available for the different management tools**

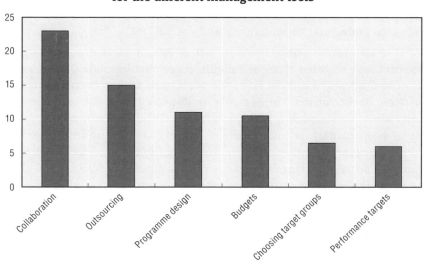

The area where local level actors appeared to have the lowest level flexibility is in the setting of eligibility criteria and performance targets. Eligibility criteria appear to be used as a tool in many countries for maintaining control and the achievement of national objectives. In Poland, for example, while local authorities within the relatively decentralised system are granted wide autonomy in creating labour market programmes, the beneficiaries of these policy interventions are strictly defined. There are six target groups identified nationally that can be supported by labour market policy, and it is almost impossible to help people not belonging to any of these groups. In Austria, while the local offices have some freedom in deciding who to support, target groups are nevertheless also defined nationally in a set of goals (which include, for example, the integration of older persons). Similarly, it is rare for local-level officers to have any flexibility in the setting of performance targets for their offices although they do in over half of all cases negotiate the targets set at higher governance levels.

Other forms of active labour market policy

It is worth reiterating that the above analysis is based on active labour market policy funded by public employment institutions in each country for those eligible for employment insurance benefits. If active labour market policy funded by other institutions (for example municipalities and other stakeholders sourcing European programmes) were to be taken into account, the picture would be slightly different. For example in Ireland, there is local input from partnerships into the work of the local employment service, in addition to the services provided by the national training and employment authority, FÁS. In Japan, local authorities develop their own employment measures which complement those managed by the Employment Security Bureau (central office), the prefectural labour bureaus and the local PES offices.

It is also important to consider active labour market policy targeted towards those on other types of benefits, given that in many OECD member countries, employment services for social assistance beneficiaries are relatively decentralised. For example, in Canada provincial and municipal social assistance covers a high proportion of the unemployed. In France entitlement to RMI (*revenu minimum d'insertion* – minimum integration revenue) is managed by *Départements*. The proportion of unemployed receiving municipal social assistance is also high in the Netherlands. As noted above, the municipalities are responsible for the implementation of subsistence benefit and tools in the area of subsidised work, and in this case the system is particularly decentralised. In a more recent development, 57 municipalities will now take the lead in bringing relevant regional labour market parties (employers, schools, UWV, CWI, etc.) together on the scale of the regional labour market to stimulate the formulation and co-ordination of regional labour market policies. These policies concern all unemployed in the region; unemployed with an unemployment insurance or disability insurance, unemployed with a social assistance benefit and those who are unemployed but receiving no benefits. Similarly, in Germany, the high proportion of long term unemployed means that many people receive active labour market support under the means tested SGB II fund, which offers considerable new flexibility for municipalities and local PES offices (often combined at the local level) to identify the right type of support required to help people back into employment.

In Denmark, active labour market policy is now administered locally in "one stop shops" co-run by Job Centres (catering for those eligible for employment insurance) and municipalities (catering for those not eligible). In 14 pilot Job Centres, the central government has delegated the responsibility for employment activities to the municipalities alone, and as of 1st August 2008 all job centres will be run by municipalities. In the new system, the social partners are also involved in planning and following-up the activities of the local Job Centres both for the insured unemployed and other local target groups. In Norway, since 2006, the *Trygdeetaten* (National Insurance Organisation), *Aetat* (PES) and the social services in the municipalities have been in a process of merger and reform under the new NAV framework (Norwegian Labour and Welfare Organisation). At the local level the new offices will provide integrated services.

In addition, even relatively centralised systems that are based on outsourcing (such as Australia) can – through the strength of market forces and the variety of providers operating – take local circumstances into account, even if local policy makers are not involved in setting local priorities. For example, private providers paid by results are likely to have an ethnic and social mix among their counsellors that matches the local population. In terms of the adaptation of the services provided to local circumstances, etc., effective quasi-market arrangements are a useful instrument of decentralisation, even when the management framework (the definition of outcomes that are rewarded) is completely national with effectively no local autonomy. Outsourced providers also have more control over the hiring and firing of staff locally. However it must be remembered that this may only lead to decentralisation in relation to service delivery, as opposed to allowing local actors the freedom to engage in planning longer term strategies in co-operation with other stakeholders.

The degree of communication between different government levels

Another factor not taken into account in the above analysis is the degree of separation between functions between different governance levels. For example, the scoring process has not differentiated between those countries where responsibility for different management functions are shared between levels, and those where they are dealt with autonomously, with little interaction between the different functions. For example in Belgium the national body ONEM is responsible for benefit administration, while regional bodies are responsible for placement, with relatively limited co-operation between the two. More recently, Belgium has now set up federal-regional agreements regarding the management of some overlapping functions to improve information flows and negotiation between the different levels.

In the light of the above caveats, while it is possible to allocate relative scores as to the flexibility of local offices administering active labour market policy for those on employment insurance in the Public Employment Service system, it would be difficult to extrapolate from this an all-purpose score for decentralisation which could be used as a basis for measuring overall decentralisation. What the analysis does show, however, is that there is some way to go before local offices at the level of local labour markets have an adequate level of flexibility to fully adapt employment policy to local needs and to priorities set in partnership with other local actors.

The need for flexibility available to other local actors

Of course it is not just labour market agencies that need to have flexibility to contribute to needs and strategies at the local level. Work is currently being conducted by the OECD LEED Programme to understand better the flexibility available to other local stakeholders (particularly in the fields of economic development and skills), and to analyse the influence that this has on local policy co-ordination and integration (OECD, 2009 forthcoming). Labour market policy, vocational training and economic development are often compartmentalised, managed in "silos" and guided by narrow objectives which poorly take into account the broader policy context.

Overall research findings show that economic development is the most flexible policy area out of the three with employment being the least. However there is some variation between the countries. In several countries – most notably Canada, New Zealand and the United States – the vocational training system is felt to be particularly inflexible and resistant to change. This reflects the fact that curricula are not easy to alter and programmes take time to establish. Institutions also have a duty to take into account demands from the local student population. In contrast, economic development policy is often guided by a number of different actors at the national level, and in many cases there is no responsible ministry at this level, leading to less national level control.

Conclusion

At the local level, it is crucial that different agencies and actors work together on the complex and cross cutting labour market issues that affect their particular community, to innovate as necessary and adapt policies to local needs. However in many cases, and despite many years of experimentation in the field of local partnerships and networking, policy integration at the local level is still failing to materialise.

To a certain extent this may be seen as the result of a failure to provide flexibility to agencies working at the level where local strategic objectives in the field of employment policy are most effectively set – the level of local labour market areas (i.e. sub-regional areas, of less than 800 000 people). The analysis of the relative flexibility of labour market policy outlined above has shown that local PES offices in many countries remain restricted in the degree to which they can influence the design of policies, move funding between budgets lines, negotiate performance objectives and choose local target groups.

Because of this, while local PES offices generally collaborate in partnership with other stakeholders and actors at the local level in OECD countries, they are perhaps sometimes only participating at face value. While these local offices will benefit from promoting their own active labour market programming to other actors, they will have little opportunity to better align these programmes to goals set in partnership.

A major factor restricting the ability of national actors to decentralise flexibility down to the local level is the need to retain accountability within the delivery of policy. Indeed, this is one of the most difficult challenges faced by governments seeking to introduce reforms in the management of their policies. Truly flexible policy delivery implies a sharing of responsibility for decision-making at the local level among a number of actors, and agreement on an accountability framework politically acceptable to the various government levels involved is rarely an easy task.

Ongoing OECD research suggests that reconciling flexibility and accountability can be best achieved by encouraging the national level to consult the local level when setting the local targets for labour market policy and vocational training (OECD, 2009). This joint review would seek to ensure that sector performances are compatible with broader area-based strategies, while preserving the integrity of the vertical accountability relationships. Strengthening horizontal accountability relationships, by encouraging social partners and economic development stakeholders to scrutinise and comment on the targets proposed, could further contribute to policy co-ordination locally. Experience suggests that greater flexibility should be allocated to those local areas which have the highest capacity to use it.

Notes

1. A Travel to Work Area or TTWA is a statistical tool used to indicate an area from where the population would generally commute to a larger town, city or conurbation for the purposes of employment.

2. Estimates of flexibility in the management of labour market policy, or of "effective decentralisation" in OECD countries have been prepared by the OECD Secretariat (LEED Programme), drawing on the results of the Questionnaire to the Employment, Labour and Social Affairs Committee (ELSAC) on Activation of Labour Market Policy in 2007. The findings were supplemented by further research in March and April 2008. No information was available for Sweden at the time of research. Colleagues in the Directorate of Employment, Labour and Social Affairs, particularly David Grubb and Peter Tergeist, should be thanked for their active support during this process and comments on the analysis. The results of the questionnaire were approved by the LEED Committee in November 2007 and further validated at the Conference on "Decentralisation and Co-ordination: The Twin Challenges of Labour Market Policy" held in Venice on 17-19th April 2008.

3. In some cases, these offices are part of the ministry itself, while in other cases they are branches of a national agency (such as *Jobcentre plus* in the UK, or ANPE on France).

4. In each case, one of three scores was awarded for each country on the basis of the degree of flexibility (1.0 flexibility, 0.5 some flexibility, 0 no flexibility). All accountability mechanisms were given equal weight in the resulting analysis, except for (e) *collaboration* and (f) *outsourcing* which were allocated a total possible score of 0.5. Where a country does not use a particular tool in managing regional or local offices, for example "management by objectives" in the case of Spain and Switzerland, this is taken into account using a normalisation process.

5. The Australian Government will be introducing a new framework for employment services nationally to commence on 1 July 2009.

Bibliography

OECD (2009, forthcoming), *Breaking Out of Silos: Joining up policy locally*, OECD Publishing, Paris.

FLEXIBLE POLICY FOR MORE AND BETTER JOBS – ISBN 978-92-64-05918-4 – © OECD 2009

ANNEX 2.A1

Table 2.A1.1. **Public Employment Service (PES) hierarchy in OECD countries[1]**

	National	Regional	Sub-Regional	Local
Austria	AMS	Regional AMS offices (9)	Local PES office (100) – combined with BIZ in 61 cases	
Australia	DEEWR Centrelink	DEEWR (7)	Region (8) additional offices in certain states	Centrelink Customer Services Centres (321)
Belgium	FOD Werkgelegenheid, Arbeid en Sociaal Overleg/SPF Emploi, Travail et Concertation Sociale, POD Maatschappelijke Integratie/ SPP Intégration Sociale, RVA/ONEM, RSZ/ONSS	Ministère de la Région de Bruxelles-Capitale/ Ministerie van het Brussels Hoofdstedelijk Gewest, Ministère de la Région Wallonne, Vlaams ministerie van Werk en Sociale Economie, Ministerium der Deutschsprachigen Gemeinschaft, FOREM, VDAB, ACTIRIS, ADG (4) ERSV (5) Coordination Inter-régionale FORUM (3) BNCTO (1)	Sub-regional employment offices (19 Flanders, 20 Wallonia), ONEM Bureau du Chômage (30), Sub-regional Employment Committees RESOC, SERR, CSEF, MIRE, BNCTO (le Comité néerlandophone bruxellois pour l'emploi et la Formation) and the CCFEE (Commission consultative pour la formation, l'emploi et l'enseignement)	ALE, Maisons de l'Emploi, Services locaux d'accueil et d'information, Espace Ressources Emploi, Carrefours Formation, Centres de compétences, Lokale Werkwinkel, Local contact points (where the ALE/PWA, VDAB are present)
Canada	Service Canada	Provincial governments (10) and territories (3)	Service Canada (320)	96 outreach and mobile sites
Czech Republic	Employment Service Administration (ESA)		Authorised labour offices at socioeconomic centres of administrative regions (14), district labour offices (77)	Detached offices (167) and branch offices (8 in Prague)
Denmark	The National Labour Market Authority (AMS)	Employment regions (4)		Job centres (77), pilot job centres (14). As of 1 August 2009 all the job centres will be managed by municipalities
Finland	Ministry of Labour		T&E Centres (district offices)	PES regional offices (101), local branch offices (45-50) and Labour Force Service Centres (39)
France	DGEFP, ANPE, AFPA, APEC	Directions régionales DRTEFP (22), ANPE offices (22), Comités paritaires régionaux de APEC (15)	Directions déléguées DDTEFP (120), Bassins d'emploi (94)	Local ANPE agencies (824), Missions locales (402), PAIO (106), points relais (154), AFPA sites de formation et de certification (265), AFPA services d'orientation professionnelle (207), Maisons de l'Emploi (227), Bassins d'Emploi (379) and Poles d'Emploi (planned for December 2008)

Table 2.A1.1. **Public Employment Service (PES) hierarchy in OECD countries[1]** (cont.)

	National	Regional	Sub-Regional	Local
Germany	Bundesagentur für Arbeit, Zentralstelle für Arbeitsvermittlung, Institute for Employment Research	Regional Directorates (10)	Local employment agencies (178)	Branch offices of the local employment agencies (660). For SGB II 353 working groups (Arbeitsgemeinschaften, ARGEn) of employment agencies and municipalities
Greece	OAED	OAED regional directorates (7)		Employment promotion centres (80) and Local employment offices (41) shortly to be combined into KPA 2 (121)
Hungary	NESO	Regional labour centres (7)	Combined Service Centres and Branch offices (19)	Local branch offices (168) and local level employment information points (393)
Ireland	FAS	FAS regional offices (8)		Employment Service Offices (70), Social welfare local offices (58) and branch offices (68), Local employment service offices (25 central offices and over 100 local outlets
Italy	Ministry of Labour and Social Security, ISFOL, Italia Lavoro	Regional government PES (15 regions, 5 autonomous governments)	Sub-regional PES offices (538)	Local PES offices (297) and part time offices (471)
Japan	Employment Security Bureau (central office), part of Ministry of Health, Labour and Welfare	Prefectural labour bureaus (47)	Local Public Employment Security offices (461)	
Korea	Ministry of Labour	Local Employment Councils	PES offices (84). In addition regional (major cities) and local labour offices (46) focusing on industrial relations. Legal basis exists for local employment councils at this level	
Netherlands	Centre for Work and Income, UWV	CWI (6) UWV (6)		CWI(127) UWV (40), municipalities (443)
New Zealand	Work and income		Work and income regional offices (11), contact centres (5)	Front line site offices (152)
Norway	Aetat (PES), Trygdeetaten (NIO)		County offices (19)	AETAT (120 local offices, 30-40 offices reduced services), Trygdeetaten (450), new merged NAV offices (280 of 460 planned by end 2009)

Table 2.A1.1. **Public Employment Service (PES) hierarchy in OECD countries**[1] (cont.)

	National	Regional	Sub-Regional	Local
Poland	Ministry of Labour and Social Affairs	WUP Wojewódzkie labour offices (16)	PUP Powiatowe labour offices (338)	
Portugal	IEFP	Regional Delegations (5) including coordination services	Job centres (86), Customer reception centres (117) Vocational training Centres (58). etc.	
Slovak Republic	LSAF			LSAF (46), outpost workplaces
Spain	INEM	Autonomous Communities (17) Basque Country, Ceuta and Melilla have integrated PES combining state and regional services		PES offices (700)
Switzerland	SECO		Cantons (26)	ORPs (131)
United Kingdom	Jobcentre Plus	Administrative regional offices (11), Benefit Delivery Centres (38, roll out in progress), Contact centres (31)		Jobcentre Plus local offices (818)
United States	Department of Labor	State Workforce Investment Boards (50)	Workforce Investment Boards (650)	One-Stop Centers (1 637), Satellite or Affiliated Sites (1 764)

1. As at 2008.

ISBN 978-92-64-05918-4
Flexible Policy for More and Better Jobs
© OECD 2009

Chapter 3

Effects of Decentralisation and Flexibility of Active Labour Market Policy on Country-Level Employment Rates[1]

by
Randall Eberts and Sylvain Giguère

This chapter examines the relationship between flexibility in the management of labour market policy and employment outcomes. The flexibility index is related statistically to factors affecting employment rates at the country level and to employment rates directly. Directly and indirectly relating the flexibility index to employment rates provides insight into the various paths that flexibility may take in affecting labour market outcomes. The econometric analysis suggests that sub-regional flexibility is positively and statistically significantly related to employment rates in the countries surveyed. One explanation is that sub-regional flexibility leads to more responsive and customised active labour market programmes, which in turn direct more training resources to those who need it, resulting in a positive effect on employment rates.

Much has been written on the benefits and costs of decentralisation, but little empirical research has been undertaken to demonstrate the link between decentralisation and labour market outcomes. One reason for the lack of empirical research is the absence of quantitative measures of decentralisation across a broad sample of countries. Chapter 2 is an attempt to fill this gap. The OECD conducted a survey of 25 countries regarding their level of flexibility (or effective decentralisation) in the management of active labour market programmes among national, regional, and local layers of government and/or administration. The survey asked the national government of each country to rate the level of flexibility available to each administrative layer with respect to:

- Designing programmes.
- Allocating budgets.
- Defining target groups.
- Setting performance criteria.
- Collaborating with other actors.
- Outsourcing.

Scores were awarded to each country for each of these six categories on the basis of flexibility and an aggregate index was constructed (see Chapter 2).

The purpose of this chapter is to examine the relationship between flexibility and labour market outcomes. The flexibility index is related statistically to factors affecting employment rates at the country level and to employment rates directly. Directly and indirectly relating the flexibility index to employment rates provides insight into the various paths that flexibility may take in affecting labour market outcomes. A country's employment rate, measured as the number of people employed divided by working age population, is one of several measures of labour market outcomes. Others include the unemployment rate, labour force participation, and employment growth. We chose the employment rate because it measures the extent to which a country's population is engaged in work, one of the functions of active labour market programmes. Furthermore, the employment rate takes into account two other measures of labour force outcomes – participation rate and unemployment rate – since participation rate and (1-unemployment rate) multiplied together equals the employment rate.

It is important to note that estimating empirical relationships between decentralisation measures and country-level labour outcome measures such as employment rates is difficult and fraught with issues of causation, aggregation bias, and the inability to detect the more subtle relationships of individuals helped by workforce programmes and the vast majority who are not part of the programmes covered under decentralisation. Furthermore, decentralisation may be more reflective of a culture or attitude toward incentives and local decision-making that is embodied in the way a country conducts its programmes than it is a direct effect on programmes and outcomes. Finally, the very small sample size of 25 countries means that any estimates will be quite imprecise. Therefore, the results should be viewed with caution. On the other hand, they provide an initial look at possible relationships between decentralisation/flexibility and employment rates.

Conceptual framework

As previously mentioned, the basic premise is that flexibility in management promotes a more effective use of workforce development services through being more responsive to the needs of workers and employers, and by encouraging more innovative approaches to meeting their needs. Flexibility can also be conducive to a better co-ordination with other policy areas such as economic development, leading to synergies and more strategic actions to be carried out, which translate into better employment outcomes (in addition to Chapter 1, see also Chapple, 2005; Giguère, 2003, 2008; Giloth, 2004; Osterman, 2005; OECD, 2009). However, these advantages may be offset by efficiency losses brought about by duplication of active labour market programmes across a country, implementation diverted from principle objectives, delays in policy implementation, and poor delivery and administration of services due to inadequate staff capabilities (see Chapter 1). An empirical analysis, in essence, weighs the pros and cons of decentralisation and provides estimates of its net effect on employment rates at the national level.

We posit a simple model that relates a local flexibility/decentralisation index to employment rates. There are several paths through which the index can influence employment rates, as depicted in Figure 3.1. The first two paths relate to active labour market programmes, principally the public employment service (PES) and job training. The third path relates to institutional factors and market characteristics that may affect the efficiency of the labour market. These factors include the flexibility of the wage determination process to respond to market shocks, the ease of hiring and firing workers, cooperation in labour relations, and female participation in the labour force may all be related to employment rates.

Figure 3.1. **Path diagram of the possible relationships between the sub-regional flexibility index and employment rate**

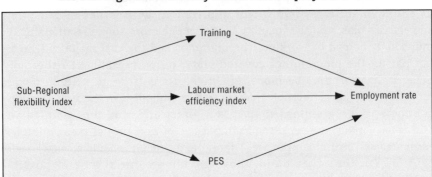

The flexibility index, which is designed to reflect the local and regional autonomy in designing and administering active labour market programmes, can affect active labour market programmes in at least two ways. The first effect is an increase in programme efficiency. More local flexibility can translate into better customised employment service delivery, and more adequate implementation of training programmes with respect to local needs. The second effect is an increase in the level of spending on public labour exchange and training programmes. Increased spending may have either a positive or neutral effect on employment rates. A positive effect could reflect the result of a better understanding of the needs of workers through decentralised decision making and administration and a concomitant increase in investment in workers to meet those identified needs. If that were the case, the increased spending on active labour market programmes should have a positive effect on employment rates. A neutral or even detrimental effect may occur if the increased spending comes about because of duplication of services, which could result from the lack of coordination by higher level units of government. In that case, the additional revenues would not lead to increased labour market outcomes.

The third path in which flexibility can influence employment rates is the effect of flexibility/decentralisation on labour market institutions and dynamics. Local flexibility in government decision making may directly affect employment rates through facilitating the formation of strong partnerships with local businesses or through direct government intervention in local labour market regulation and processes. Local flexibility may have an indirect effect as well, by reflecting the general attitude toward local autonomy in decision making that may also permeate institutions and the functioning of local labour markets.

Survey questions

As outlined in Chapter 2, the survey was administered to 25 OECD countries, which had regional or local administrative entities of sufficient size to be able to carry out the six functions related to the design, implementation, and administration of workforce development services. Using nomenclature developed by the European Union and adopted by the OECD, the survey distinguishes among three levels: 1) administrative regions with a population between 800 000 and 3 million; 2) sub-regions with a population between 150 000 and 800 000; and 3) localities under 150 000.

Table 3.1 displays the survey responses for the six categories for each level by country. The categories receiving the highest marks for flexibility and decentralisation are collaboration with other actors and outsourcing. The categories scoring the lower points for flexibility are "defining target groups" and "setting performance criteria". The correlations of the responses regarding local and regional flexibility within each of the six categories provide interesting insights as to tradeoffs between flexibility at those two levels. For instance, the low correlation between regional and local entities in allocating budgets suggests that one or the other, not both, are given that authority. On the other hand, the higher correlation for outsourcing suggests that it is more often the case that both the local and regional entities outsource services. Therefore, for some aspects of decentralisation, regional and local entities are similar in the extent to which they have authority to exercise responsibility for those functions, whereas for other functions, their authority differs.

It is also interesting to examine the correlations across functions by level of government, particularly within regional and local entities. Table 3.2 displays the correlations across functions at the regional level. In each case, we see that the degree of decentralisation of functions at the regional level or at the local level varies. For example, at the regional level, decentralisation of designing programmes and allocating budgets is highly correlated (0.69). The same high correlation is evident between allocating budgets and setting performance criteria and between defining target groups and setting performance criteria. On the other hand, collaborating and outsourcing are negatively related to designing programmes, which indicates that those regional entities that are given authority to do the former do not engage in the latter two functions. Correlations at the local level show somewhat similar patterns but the relationships are not as strong. One exception is the strong positive correlation between designing programmes and outsourcing (0.38). The other is outsourcing and allocating budgets. At the regional level the first relationship is negative and the second quite weak, suggesting that local entities may need to outsource services because they have less capacity than regional entities.

Table 3.1. **Survey responses by country, category and regional and local entities**

	Designing programmes		Allocating budgets		Defining target groups		Setting performance criteria		Collaborating		Outsourcing	
	Regional	Local	Regional	Local	Regional	Local	Regional	Local	Regional	Local	Regional	Local
Australia	0.5	0	0	0	0	0	0	0	1	1	1	0
Austria	0.5	0.5	0.5	1	0	0.5	0.5	0.5	1	1	1	0
Belgium	1	0.5	1	0	0	0	1	0	1	1	1	0
Canada	0.5	0	0.5	0.5	0.5	0	0.5	0.5	1	1	1	1
Czech Republic	0.5	0.5	0	0.5	0	1	0	0.5	0	1	0	1
Denmark	0	1	0.5	1	0	0.5	0.5	0.5	1	1	1	1
Finland	n.a.	1	n.a.	0.5	n.a.	0.5	n.a.	0.5	n.a.	1	n.a.	1
France	0.5	0.5	0	0.5	0	0	0.5	0	1	1	1	1
Germany	0.5	0.5	0	0.5	0	0.5	0.5	0.5	1	1	1	1
Greece	0	0	0	0	0	0	0	0	1	1	0	0
Hungary	1	0.5	1	0	0	0.5	0.5	0	1	1	0	0
Ireland	n.a.	0.5	n.a.	0.5	n.a.	0	n.a.	0.5	n.a.	1	n.a.	1
Italy	1	0	1	0.5	1	0.5	1	0	1	1	1	1
Japan	0.5	0.5	1	0	0.5	0.5	0.5	0.5	1	0	1	1
Korea	0.5	0.5	0.5	0.5	0	0.5	0	0.5	1	1	0	0
Netherlands	0.5	0.5	0.5	0	0	0	0	0	1	1	1	0
New Zealand	n.a.	0.5	n.a.	0.5	n.a.	0.5	n.a.	0.5	n.a.	1	n.a.	1
Norway	0	0.5	0	0.5	0	0	0	0	1	1	1	1
Poland	1	1	1	1	0	0	1	0	1	1	1	1
Portugal	0	0	0.5	0.5	0	0	0.5	0.5	1	1	1	1
Slovak Republic	0	0.5	0	0	0	0	0	0	1	0	1	0
Spain	0.5	0	0.5	0	1	0	1	0	1	1	1	0
Switzerland	n.a.	1	n.a.	1	n.a.	0	n.a.	n.a.	n.a.	1	n.a.	1
United Kingdom	0	0	0	0.5	0	0	0	0	1	1	1	0
United States	0.5	0.5	0.5	0.5	1	1	1	0.5	1	1	1	1
Sum	9.5	11	9	10.5	4	6.5	9	6	20	23	17	15
Correlation	0.174	0.026	0.279	0.036	−0.073	0.266						

Source: OECD Decentralisation and Flexibility Survey (see Chapter 2).

From an econometric perspective, the relatively high correlation among some functions, both across governmental layers and across functions within governmental layers would make it difficult to distinguish between the effects of regional and local practices on labour market outcomes. The correlation also makes it to difficult to examine the individual effects of specific workforce functions on labour market outcomes. Therefore, we have employed an index – the sub-regional flexibility index – that aggregates these effects but still captures the overall extent to which the various functions involved in delivering workforce services are decentralised.

FLEXIBLE POLICY FOR MORE AND BETTER JOBS – ISBN 978-92-64-05918-4 – © OECD 2009

Table 3.2. **Correlations across functions at the regional and local levels**

	Designing programmes	Allocating budgets	Defining target groups	Setting performance criteria	Collaborating	Outsourcing
Regional level						
Designing programmes	1.00					
Allocating budgets	0.69	1.00				
Defining target groups	0.27	0.35	1.00			
Setting performance criteria	0.60	0.68	0.61	1.00		
Collaborating	−0.03	0.25	0.12	0.25	1.00	
Outsourcing	−0.07	0.07	0.26	0.38	0.46	1.00
Local level						
Designing programmes	1.00					
Allocating budgets	0.43	1.00				
Defining target groups	0.33	0.27	1.00			
Setting performance criteria	0.27	0.45	0.58	1.00		
Collaborating	−0.08	0.37	0.02	0.00	1.00	
Outsourcing	0.32	0.51	0.32	0.51	0.05	1.00

Chapter 2 has explained how the sub-regional index was built, aggregated across functions with collaboration and outsourcing each given half weights. The sub-regional index presents a number of advantages over the regional index for the quality of the data: i) data population is greater as not all countries have a regional level (with more than 800 000 inhabitants); ii) the sub-regional index adds up flexibility at two possible governance levels, depending on the country – the local (up to 150 000 inhabitants) and the sub-regional properly speaking (between 150 000 and 800 000 inhabitants); and iii) the sub-regional level is widely viewed as the one that corresponds to local labour markets or travel-to-work areas, where labour market, skills and economic conditions are rather homogenous and susceptible to trigger differentiated decisions as regards workforce development. In contrast, administrative regions often comprise far greater populations and present a diversity of economic and social contexts.

Estimation results

The path diagram, depicted in Figure 3.1, can be described by four equations. The first equation relates employment rates (ER) to training expenditures per GDP (T), public employment service expenditures per GDP (P), and an index of labour market efficiency (Q):

$$ER = \alpha T + \beta P + \gamma Q + \delta Z + \varepsilon \qquad [1]$$

where Z includes other variables not related to T, P, or Q that may also affect ER. As described by the path diagram, the sub-regional flexibility index (S) may affect ER either directly or through the three factors. In the first case, S would be included in Equation [1] along with the other variables shown. It may also be included as an interaction term with each of the three factors to reflect the enhanced effect of these factors on employment rates with greater local flexibility. We leave these two alternative specifications – including the sub-regional flexibility index entered directly into the equation and interactively – out of Equation [1], because preliminary estimates found that these effects were statistically insignificant.

In the second case, we would include a separate equation for each of the three factors with S included as one of the explanatory variables. Thus,

$$T = a_0 + a_1S + b_2Z_T + e_T \qquad [2]$$

$$P = b_0 + b_1S + b_2Z_P + e_P \qquad [3]$$

$$Q = c_0 + c_1S + c_2Z_Q + e_Q \qquad [4]$$

where the Zs are additional exogenous variables not related to S, but related to the each of the three factors.

One can see from these four equations that S is modelled to directly affect the three factors, which in turn affect ER. This can be seen by substituting the equation for each of the factors (Equations [2] to [4]) for the respective variable in Equation [1]. This yields a reduced-form equation that relates S to ER without explicitly stating the intervening effects. However, the magnitude of the indirect effect is stated by the combination of coefficients associated with S in Equations [2]-[4] and the coefficients of the respective factors in Equation [1]. Thus, the reduced form effect of S on ER is:

$$\alpha a_1 + \beta b_1 + \gamma c_1$$

Each equation can be estimated separately using OLS. However, it may be the case that the error terms, particularly in Equations [2]-[4], are correlated. This may occur because of unmeasured factors, such as a country's attitude toward local autonomy or because of the country's underlying propensity toward publicly provided employment services.[2] Therefore, seemingly unrelated regression estimation is appropriate and will be used as an alternative method of estimation.

In order to estimate the set of equations, we use variables from the OECD and the World Economic Forum. Variables for the employment rate, public employment service (expenditures as a percentage of GDP), job training (expenditures as a percentage of GDP), GDP, population, and regional disparity are from the OECD data base. The index derived from the flexibility/decentralisation survey has been previously described.

The labour market efficiency index was constructed by the World Economic Forum for its annual global competitiveness index. The index takes into account the factors that include labour productivity, non-wage labour costs, brain drain and the use of professional human resource specialists, which overall reflect the degree to which labour markets equilibrate supply and demand, and human resources are used productively[3] (*World Economic Forum*, 2008).

Table 3.3 shows pair wise correlations among the various key factors. Statistical correlations suggest a strong relationship between sub-regional flexibility and job training and between sub-regional flexibility and the labour market efficiency index. Because of the strong correlation between the sub-regional flexibility index and the labour market efficiency index, including both in a regression that explains employment rates may result in imprecise and statistically insignificant regression coefficients, even when the two variables are jointly statistically significant.

Table 3.3. **Correlation among employment rates and selected factors**

	Employment rate	PES	Job training	Labour market efficiency index	Sub-regional flexibility index	Mean	Min.	Max.
Employment rate	1.00					0.667	0.53	0.77
PES	0.45	1.00				0.16	0.01	0.49
Job training	0.37	0.27	1.00			0.17	0.01	0.51
Labour Market Efficiency Index	0.74	0.20	0.05	1.00		4.7	3.5	5.7
Sub-regional Flexibility Index	0.31	−0.14	0.46	0.43	1.00	2.16	0.5	4.0

Using this structure, we first regress employment rates on public employment services (PES), job training and the labour market efficiency index, along with other exogenous variables.[4] These results are shown in Table 3.4. We find that all three factors have a strong and statistically significant relationship with employment rate. For instance, a one point increase in the labour market efficiency index is associated with a 7.37 percentage point increase in a country's employment rate, holding the other factors constant.[5] An increase in job training expenditures per GDP of 0.1 percentage point is associated with a 1.22 percentage point increase in the employment rate.[6] That is, considering both variables to be at their mean values, an increase from 0.17% of GDP to 0.27% of GDP in training expenditures is associated with an increase from 66.7% to 67.9% in the employment rate. An increase in PES expenditures per GDP by the same magnitude has a similar effect on employment rates. Referring to the beta coefficients of these three factors offers a perspective on their relative effects. A *beta* coefficient is a unit-less measure of the effect of a change of one standard deviation in the explanatory variable on the dependent variable. For example, an increase of

Table 3.4. **Estimates of factors affecting employment rates**

Explanatory variables	Mean	Employment rate 2005		Training	Public employment service (PES)	Labour Market Efficiency Index
		Equation [1]		Equation [2]	Equation [3]	Equation [4]
		Coeff/(t-stat)	Beta	Coeff/(t-stat)	Coeff/(t-stat)	Coeff/(t-stat)
PES	0.16	13.44 (2.24)	0.23			
Training	0.17	12.23 (2.20)	0.25			
Labour market efficiency index	4.7	7.37 (3.12)	0.64			
Sub-regional flexibility index	2.2			0.047 (2.20)	−0.029 (−1.49)	0.198 (2.17)
Tax rate (%)	38.1	−0.19 (−2.33)	−0.29			
Employment Protection Legislation	1.89	2.32 (1.85)	0.33			
Product market regulation	2.03	−2.11 (−1.71)	−0.21			
Per capita GDP 2000 (USD 1 000)				0.008 (2.28)		
Unemployment rate 2000	7.12				−0.014 (−2.64)	
Regional disparity	0.18					−3.26 (−2.03)
Constant		34.29 (2.15)		−0.11 (−1.26)	0.33 (4.77)	4.85 (12.89)
Adj. R-square		0.78		0.31	0.19	0.25
Observations		25		25	25	25

Note: Estimates are derived from ordinary least squares regression. T-statistics are in parentheses. The mean of the dependent variable (employment rate) is 66.7 with a minimum of 53.0 and a maximum of 77.2.

one standard deviation in the share of GDP spent on job training is associated with a change of 0.25 standard deviations in the employment rate. An increase of one standard deviation in the share of GDP spent on public employment services has a similar effect – a change of 0.23 standard deviations in the employment rate. The effect of labour market efficiency index is more than double that of training and PES, however.

The next step is to estimate the effect of sub-regional flexibility on the three factors included in Equation [1]. Separate regressions show that sub-regional flexibility is statistically significantly related to job training and labour market efficiency, but not PES. The results are shown the columns labelled Equations [2]-[4] in Table 3.4. Estimates show that an increase of

1.0 point in the sub-regional flexibility index is associated with an increase of 0.047 percentage points in training expenditures per GDP and an increase of 0.20 points in the labour market efficiency index. The corresponding *beta* coefficients are 0.38 and 0.39, respectively. The correlation between PES and the sub-regional flexibility index is not statistically significant. For training, the estimates suggest that an increase in sub-regional flexibility (through devolving responsibilities to local levels) is associated with an increase in nationwide expenditures on training as a share of GDP. The results could be explained by the possibility that local areas, by being closer to customers, are better able to understand the needs of customers and therefore design programmes that offer more targeted training, increasing the overall expenditure on training for a country. It may also be the case that duplication of services across local entities has also increased expenditures. Whether or not the increase in job training is beneficial depends on the effect of job training on labour market outcomes, which from the first stage regression is positive.[7]

Combining the effects of the sub-regional flexibility index on these two factors and then relating the separate effects of training and the labour market efficiency index on employment rates yields the following relationship: an increase of 1 point in the sub-regional flexibility index is associated with a 2.03 percentage point increase in the employment rate. Including the coefficient associated with PES, even though it is not statistically significant, lowers the combined estimate to 1.64 percentage points. By comparison, directly relating sub-regional flexibility to employment rates yields an estimate that is slightly higher; an increase of 1 point in the sub-regional flexibility index is associated with a 2.30 percentage points increase in employment rates. The coefficient is statistically significant, with a t-statistic of 2.75.[8] A generous interpretation of the difference in these two results – 1.64 and 2.30 – is that sub-regional flexibility is associated with a larger increase in employment rates than what would come about from a direct increase in expenditures in job training and an increase in labour market efficiency, even when taking into account the negative effect of sub-regional flexibility on PES expenditures. This suggests the possibility that sub-regional flexibility enhances the effectiveness of job training and PES services. However, this possible effect needs much more detailed examination before such a conclusion can be reached.[9]

Discussion

Estimates suggest that sub-regional flexibility is positively and statistically significantly related to employment rates in the countries surveyed by the OECD. An increase of 1 point in the flexibility index (for an index that ranges from 0 to 5.0) is related to an increase in employment rates of 1.64 percentage points, and an increase of 2.03 percentage points if PES is omitted from the estimation. The results appear to be robust across different methods of estimation, such as OLS and seemingly unrelated regression. Furthermore, the results are close to the reduced-form estimate when the sub-regional flexibility index is entered directly in Equation [1] instead of the training, PES and labour market efficiency index variables. However, one must be cautioned not to draw definitive conclusions from these estimates. Since the estimates are based on cross-sectional country-level data, it is not possible to infer causal relationships. Rather, these estimates should be interpreted only as correlations.

Yet, these correlations suggest several possible scenarios, which warrant further investigation. One possible explanation is that sub-regional flexibility leads to more responsive and customised active labour market programmes, which in turn direct more training resources to those who need it, resulting in a positive effect on employment rates. The fact that the data used in the analysis measures flexibility at a rather disaggregate level, corresponding to local labour markets as opposed to the more diversified regional level (which often corresponds to large and populous entities), seems to support that explanation. Another explanation is that a country's move toward decentralisation and the conscious desire to devolve programmatic responsibility to local entities is manifested in more effective active labour market programmes and through institutions that lead to more efficient labour markets, as reflected in the labour market efficiency index. This second explanation steps back from a direct causal relationship between sub-regional flexibility to employment rates and hypothesises that flexibility in policy management, effective implementation of workforce development programmes and efficient markets are all three reflective of society's desire to put more responsibility in the hands of local workforce entities and give more autonomy to individual market participants to pursue their own interests. Other explanations are also possible, since the estimation is based on correlations and not causal relationships.

Needless to say, additional analysis must be conducted before one can conclude with confidence the effect of decentralisation and flexibility at the regional and local levels on labour market outcomes. Nonetheless, the results do offer guidance in pursing more in-depth analyses of the effects of decentralisation and flexibility on a country's workforce development system. To obtain more definitive results, the analysis needs to focus on individual worker data and to examine more closely the ways in which the workforce system operates at the regional and local levels. Yet, the OECD LEED survey and the ability to relate it to country-level labour market outcome measures provide the first important step toward a better understanding of the benefits of decentralisation and flexibility on the workforce system.

Notes

1. The authors thank David Balducchi, Timothy Bartik, David Grubb, Kevin Hollenbeck, Paul Swaim and Steve Wandner for their helpful comments and suggestions.

2. In the first case, S would also be correlated with the error term in each equation, introducing the possibility of a biased estimate of S on each of the three factors, T, P, and Q.

3. Each country is assigned a value from 1 to 7, based on the aggregation of the 10 components of the labour market efficiency index, which are: cooperation in labour-employer relations, flexibility of wage determination, non-wage labour costs, rigidity of employment, hiring and firing practices, firing costs, pay and productivity, reliance on professional management, brain drain and female participation in labour force. The data to derive this index come from hard data, mostly from the World Bank, as well as opinion surveys administered by the World Economic Forum.

4. The other exogenous variables include measures that capture a country's general policies and institutions that could have an effect on employment rates. These variables are taken from previous research that relates country-level policies and institutions on employment rates, as described in Chapter 7 of the *OECD Employment Outlook* (2006) and in more detail in Bassanini and Duval (2006). These variables include the UI benefit average replacement rate, average tax rates, union density, the strictness of the employment protection legislation, and product market regulation. These variables are obtained or derived from the OECD statistical data base. As shown in Table 3.4, the signs of the coefficients are mostly as expected, with the exception of the employment protection legislation, which is positive but not statistically significant at a reasonable confidence level. However, comparing our results with those found in the *OECD Employment Outlook* (2006, p. 231), we find that the sign of the employment protection legislation coefficient varies with subgroup populations. Older workers and part-time prime-wage women are positively affected by an increase in the strictness of this set of legislation. Therefore, considering the mix of negative and positive effects on the employment rates of different subgroups, its effect on the overall employment rate could be positive or at least not statistically significant. We are grateful to Paul Swaim for suggesting these additional exogenous variables.
Unlike much of the previous research, we use only cross-sectional country data since the flexibility survey was administered only once and thus the index is time-invariant. We did enter employment rates in 1995 as an explanatory variable to look at the effects of the same variables on changes in employment rates, which is what the fixed effect models in essence estimates. The results are similar, except that the coefficient of the labour market efficiency variable is much smaller and not statistically significant. Since there is no particular date in which flexibility was introduced into these countries, it does not make as much sense to think about it as affecting change in employment rates as it does to think about it reflecting a general attitude toward flexibility and local decision making.

5. Since the labour market efficiency index includes a measure of productivity, it could be the case that employment rates affect labour productivity, introducing endogeneity into Equation [1], as evidenced by results shown in Chapter 2 of the *OECD Employment Outlook* (2006). However, this possibility may be negligible since productivity is only one of 10 components in the labour market efficiency index and it is derived from an opinion survey not hard productivity data.

6. This estimate of the effect of job training on employment rates is close to what Bassanini and Duval (2006) found in their estimates for prime age males.

71

Estimates were lower for females and higher for older workers and youth – subgroups that we did not separate out in this analysis. They also used a panel data set of employment rates that stretched nearly three decades. However, since employment rates are relatively constant over time, particularly in developed countries, it is not surprising that the estimates are similar.

7. As previously mentioned, the error terms of the system of equations may be correlated, particularly the error terms in Equations [2] to [4], yielding inefficient estimates. Re-estimating the system of equations using seemingly unrelated regression methods yielded little difference in the precision of the estimates.

8. This result was derived from estimating Equation [1] with the sub-regional flexibility index substituted for the PES, training and labour market efficiency variable. The tax rate, employment protection legislation, and product market regulation variables were also included.

9. Another approach to estimating the indirect effects of sub-regional flexibility on employment rates is to interact the sub-regional flexibility index with the PES, training, and labour market efficiency variables. We tried this approach, and none of the coefficients on the interaction terms was statistically significant. The coefficient on the labour market efficiency variable was positive, while the other two were negative.

Bibliography

Bassanini, A. and R. Duval (2006), "Employment Patterns in OECD Countries: Reassessing the Role of Policies and Institutions," Social, Employment and Migration Working Papers No. 35, Directorate for Employment, Labour and Social Affairs, Employment, Labour and Social Affairs Committee, OECD, Paris.

Chapple, K. (2005), "Building Institutions from the Region Up: Regional Workforce Development Collaboratives in California", University of California, Berkeley, CA.

Giguère, S. (2003), "Managing Decentralisation and New forms of Governance", in OECD, Managing Decentralisation. A New Role for Labour Market Policy, OECD Publishing, Paris.

Giguère, S. (2008), "A Broader Agenda for Workforce Development", in OECD (2008), More than Just Jobs: Workforce Development in a Skills-based Economy, OECD Publishing, Paris.

Giloth, R.P. (2004), Workforce Development Politics: Civic Capacity and Performance, Temple University Press, Philadelphia.

OECD (2006), Employment Outlook, OECD Publishing, Paris.

OECD (2008), More than Just Jobs: Workforce Development in a Skills-based Economy, OECD Publishing, Paris.

Osterman, P. (2005), "Employment and Training Policies: New Directions for Less Skilled Adults", paper prepared for Urban Institute Conference "Workforce Policies for the Next Decade and Beyond", October, MIT Sloan School, Boston.

World Economic Forum (2008), The Global Competitiveness Report 2008-09, World Economic Forum, Geneva.

ISBN 978-92-64-05918-4
Flexible Policy for More and Better Jobs
© OECD 2009

Chapter 4

The Trade-off between Flexibility and Accountability in Labour Market Policy

by

Hugh Mosley

Labour market policy is in most countries a national priority that requires national co-ordination. Its perceived importance and the financial volume of expenditure for labour market policy place limits on the degree of flexibility for regional or local actors that is politically acceptable. Moreover, potential conflicts of interest between local and national employment service actors are an important justification for centralised rules and regulations in labour market policy. Decentralised systems frequently face problems in performance accountability due in particular to the number of organisations involved and the lack of standardisation in labour market and performance data available.

Introduction

This chapter examines trends in decentralisation and trade-offs between flexibility and accountability in the recent experience of OECD countries. The first section surveys arguments and issues in debates on decentralisation, identifies different types of decentralisation and defines basic elements of decentralisation strategies that increase regional and local flexibility in policy implementation. The second section discusses accountability criteria and types of trade-offs between decentralisation and accountability. The third, fourth and fifth sections discuss patterns of cross-national variation in key elements of local flexibility, the relationship between decentralisation and local policy co-ordination and the need for complementary capacity building strategies at the regional and local level. The final section presents conclusions and recommendations.

Decentralisation

In the most general terms decentralisation is the transfer of decision-making power and responsibility over policies from the national to the regional, sub-regional or local level (see de Vries, 2000, for a general discussion). Decentralisation in the sense used here is applicable above all to the different levels of government or administration in public or quasi-public sector (*e.g.* social insurance institutions in many countries). By contrast "deregulation", another form of flexibility, removes issues from direct public regulation and leaves their determination to the market or actors in civil society, for example, in the case of employment contracts in the labour market. Although labour law and labour market regulation have been liberalised in OECD countries in the past two decades, a common national framework has been maintained.

In these past two decades there has been a strong trend toward decentralisation in labour market policies, which has been documented by discussions and conferences at the OECD level (OECD, 1999a; OECD, 2003). The results of the first Venice Conference of 1998 and the Warsaw Conference in 2003 show clearly that decentralisation is a complex and multifaceted process that can improve policy implementation but can also have undesirable negative effects (*e.g.* duplication and fragmentation of activities, localism, uneven quality of programmes and administration).

Decentralisation trends in labour market policy reflect an increased perception of the territorial dimension of labour market policy and the need to facilitate greater co-operation with other local actors (*e.g.* Sweden, Denmark, Germany) but also broader national patterns and trends in public administration ("New Public Management") and in the division of powers between central and sub-national authorities, of which labour market policy is only one affected area.

Decentralisation arguments and issues

It is useful to consider typical arguments for and against decentralisation, not forgetting that decentralisation issues in most countries are inevitably intensely political: "some actors lose and others gain power" (Rhodes, 1981). The theoretical literature suggests that decentralisation may under certain circumstances enhance policy delivery but may also have unintended negative effects. Moreover, the theoretical benefits may be constrained in practice by other factors. A recent comparative survey of public policy discussions on this issue concludes paradoxically that "neither the theoretical arguments in favour of decentralisation, nor the arguments in favour of centralisation are convincing" and that there is not a long-term trend toward decentralisation but rather "ongoing cycles in which trends and taking sides in the discussion succeed one another continuously" (de Vries, 2000).

A number of pros and cons for decentralisation can be identified:

1. *Flexibility* vs. *equal treatment:* A classic argument for decentralisation in labour market policy is that it makes possible more tailor-made policies better adapted to local needs, in contrast to standardised national policies: "decentralisation leads to greater variety in the provision of public goods, which are tailored to better suit local populations" (Tiebout, 1956). A key question here is surely in what respects variety in public policy is desirable or acceptable and what policies should be uniform throughout the country. The strength of the argument for variety in the delivery of pubic goods would seem to depend on the size of the country and the diversity of local needs. The strongest case for decentralisation would seem to be for flexible delivery of tailor-made strategies within a national policy framework. Moreover, insofar as decentralisation entails different policies or differences in the administration of national laws in different parts of a country, it may conflict with strong notions of equal citizenship and equal application of the law, especially in countries with a strong tradition of social rights, for example, as in Germany or the Netherlands (see de Vries, 2000; Sol and Westerveld, 2005).

Within the field of labour market policy the movement toward decentralisation has been concentrated in particular in the area of active labour market policies, whereas benefit systems remain centrally regulated and, with some exceptions (*e.g.* United States and Canada), centrally administered. With regard to decentralisation of active measures it is important to distinguish between policies and implementation. Even in countries with relatively decentralised delivery systems there is usually a strong effort to retain an overall common policy framework and accountability standards (*e.g.* United States, Spain).

2. *Variety* vs. *accountability*: Decentralisation is said to promote innovation through competition between different regional and local authorities out of which best practice may emerge. Greater variation in policies and delivery systems can certainly be expected in the absence of central direction. There may be, however, offsetting negative effects in terms of duplication and reinventing the wheel and extreme outliers in performance. There would thus seem to be a strong argument for minimum quality standards and dissemination of information on best practice.

Where there is economic competition or a common market (*e.g.* in the United States or the European Union) and unregulated competition between regions (or states) lack of central regulation may lead to an undesirable negative downward spiral and "beggar thy neighbour policies", for example, in welfare and environmental policies, due to competitive pressures. Again there seems to be a strong argument for minimum standards in decentralised and competitive regimes.

3. *Capabilities*: Advocates of decentralisation argue that local actors and local decision-makers know local circumstances and needs best, whereas critics argue that familiarity with local circumstances is an asset but not a sufficient basis for analysing local needs and developing appropriate local strategies. Local political leaders and administrators may be less able and experienced. Decentralised regimes may be less likely to attract high quality personnel since the financial rewards and prestige are as a rule lower that at the central level (Prud'homme, 1995; Tanzi, 1996). Because regional and local authorities may, at least initially, lack the experience and organisational capabilities required for assuming a larger role, decentralisation needs to go hand in hand with capacity building.

4. *Political accountability*: Finally, it is frequently claimed that dispersion of decision-making power increases accountability of local (elected) policy makers in contrast to more centralised and bureaucratic administrative systems: "Locally elected authorities are more likely to reflect local preferences than are the localised centres of central government" (Ranson and Stuart, 1994). Intuitively appealing, the strength of this argument in practice may be weaker since more prestigious and powerful national officeholders may be subjected to more intensive press and public scrutiny

than are regional and local officials. In many countries turnout in local elections is significantly lower than in national elections. (de Vries, 2000; Prud'homme, 1995; Fisman and Gatti, 2002). Moreover, decentralisation of responsibility for policies to regional and local authorities may have the effect of removing important issues from the national political agenda since by definition it curtails or eliminates the possibility of national political action.

Types of decentralisation

We can observe two major types of decentralisation in OECD countries: administrative and political decentralisation (Mosley, 2003). The former represents a form of organisational flexibility within a national public employment service (PES) that is basically managerial rather than political. Bureaucratic managers in regional and local offices are delegated increased operative responsibilities by the headquarters in implementing national policy objectives (*e.g.* "management by objectives", or MBO in France, the United Kingdom or in most Scandinavian countries). Here the major influence has been the public service reform movement and "new public management" ideas, which advocate greater flexibility for the regional and local or public employment services in the context of a shift toward management by objectives.

Political decentralisation, or devolution, entails not only managerial discretion but a more far-reaching delegation of responsibility for labour market policies from the national to the sub-national (regional, state, or municipal) levels of government (*e.g.* Belgium, Canada, Denmark, Italy, Mexico, Spain, the United States). In this case the implementing organisations are not merely subordinate units of a national administration but relatively independent political entities with their own elected leadership. In such complex and multilevel governance structures the relationship between central and regional or local authorities is less hierarchical and more negotiated.

Another major trend in the provision of labour market services, and a special case, is privatisation through contracting out, or even the creation of entire "quasi-markets" (*e.g.* the Netherlands and Australia). In contrast to decentralisation within the public sector service, provision in this case is shifted to external providers. We focus in this paper on the first two forms of decentralisation and accompanying problems of reconciling decentralisation with accountability.

Administrative decentralisation

Management by objectives (also known as "management by results") is the common denominator of diverse administrative reforms in the traditions of "new public management" that aim to enhance the efficiency and effectiveness of labour market policy. Typically it entails the following elements (Mosley, 2003; Mosley, Schütz and Breyer, 2001):

1. The definition of a limited number of organisational goals and corresponding performance indicators.

2. Delegation of these performance targets to subordinate levels of the organisation.

3. Flexibility in the sense of a low density of generally binding bureaucratic rules and procedures. Managers and operating units at regional and local levels are relatively free in their choice of strategies and programmes to achieve the agreed performance targets for their units.

4. Monitoring and controlling of performance against targets. In contrast to traditional bureaucratic administration, the emphasis is on outputs or outcomes against targets rather than on controlling inputs and adherence to detailed regulations.

Sweden and Norway have the longest experience with MBO-systems in Europe, which were first introduced in the mid 1980s. Use of management by objectives in some form is now widespread in EU (European Union) public employment service organisations. This is a consequence, in the first instance, of the dissemination of performance management in the public sector in the 1980s and 1990s and within Europe by the influence of EU employment policy. Most PES organisations in EU countries now use some form of MBO in the management of their PES organisations. Outside of Europe this approach to public sector management appears to be strongest in the United States, Canada, Australia and New Zealand.

Whether MBO management systems actually lead to decentralisation and enhanced flexibility in the regional or local implementation of labour market policies is disputed. In principle MBO within a national PES organisation represents not an abandonment of central direction of the PES organisation but rather a refinement. The central PES organisation sets, on the basis of a national contract with the responsible ministry, overall goals and operational targets that are then adapted to local circumstances and can be flexibly implemented at the local level. Operating units are typically given a great deal more discretion in the use of funds and personnel and in the mix and management of programmes than in more traditional administrative structures but are expected to achieve centrally set targets or goals in terms of which their performance is assessed.

What this means in practice for decentralisation and local flexibility in implementation can vary greatly. In practice one can observe two clearly different models of performance management in MBO-type PES organisations: the more centralised and hierarchical agency model (*e.g.* France, Great Britain) and the more decentralised self-administration model (*e.g.* Austria, Germany).

The agency model entails a strong separation between policy and implementation, a national level agency agreement, top-down allocation of targets to the regions and local agencies, central controlling, etc. Thus, in France the implementation of employment policies remains relatively centralised even after the introduction of management by objectives and some developments in the direction of decentralisation. In particular the placement agency (ANPE) exhibits a top-down management style, although the impact of decentralisation has been greater in other components of the Public Employment Service. Local actors can choose from a tool box of relatively rigidly defined national programmes but they are not free to adapt them to local needs or invent new programmes. Moreover, their freedom to allocate expenditure among different types of programmes is limited (Simonin, 2003).

In Germany, the Federal Employment Service is a quasi-independent administrative agency under the jurisdiction of the Federal Ministry for Labour and Social Affairs and the 178 local PES district agencies function with a great deal of discretion in implementation, within the budgetary and legal framework established by the national employment service and social security law. The PES agency itself enjoys greater policy autonomy *vis-à-vis* the ministerial level, target setting incorporates stronger elements of dialogue, some targets are autonomously set at the regional level, and quantitative targets are only one element in a more consultative style of performance assessment; local PES agencies receive a flexible reintegration budget in deciding on their programme mix but have only limited discretion in developing their own innovative programmes.

Political decentralisation

In political decentralisation or devolution other lower tiers of government in the public sector come to play a central role in the implementation of labour market policies. Political decentralisation is strongest in federal systems in which responsibility for labour market policy is devolved to state or provincial governments that are politically, administratively and financially strongly independent actors in the national politico-administrative system, for example, in the United States or Canada.

The devolution of responsibility for the design and delivery of active labour market programmes from the central to the provincial governments in Canada is particularly interesting because it is asymmetrical. Since 1996 the responsible national ministry has concluded bilateral Labour Market Development Agreements with the provinces and territories (Box 4.1).

Through the bilateral agreements with the provinces and territories the federal government strives to maintain a national policy framework. The

Box 4.1. **Decentralisation through labour market agreements in Canada**

1. **Labour Market Development Agreements** introduced by the Employment Insurance Reform of 1996 transfer responsibility for the delivery of programmes for the insured unemployed to provincial and territorial authorities. They take two basic forms:

   ● Transfer agreements: The provinces and territories assume responsibility for the design, delivery and management of national employment and training service programmes, which continue to be funded by the federal government, insofar as they are similar to the national programmes and consistent with the purpose and guidelines of national legislation. Federal and provincial programmes are integrated in a joint employment service system.

   ● Co-management agreements: The national ministry (Human Resource and Skills Development Canada) delivers unemployment benefits and active measures but shares responsibility for their design, management and evaluation with the province.

2. **Labour Market Partnership Agreements** are a new type of bilateral federal-provincial agreement since 2005 for the delivery of services to the uninsured unemployed (*e.g.* women immigrants, young people):

   ● Response to contemporary problems of an aging population, increased regional diversity and underrepresentation of some groups in a skills-based economy with low unemployment and strong growth.

   ● Federal-provincial partnerships within a multi-year framework that grant a high degree of flexibility in programme design.

   ● Provide integrated service delivery.

   ● Have a strong accountability framework.

   Source: Jackson, 2008.

agreements specify in general terms requirements pertaining to fiscal and performance accountability, including core indicators and evaluation, integrated service provision, the co-ordination of a national labour exchange systems and the collection and dissemination of labour market information.[1] A LMDA Management Committee in which provincial and federal governments are equally represented provides for ongoing co-ordination and interpretation of the agreements.

For example, the 2005 Canada-Ontario Labour Market Development Agreement defines the shared labour market goals and objectives of the parties; sets joint priority areas and desired outcomes for the use of federal fund; provides for the establishment of an accountability framework and data sharing. A Canada-Ontario Strategic Planning Committee, which reaches it decisions on the basis of consensus, was established to oversee the bilateral agreement. The agreed level of federal funding by priority area is set out for a six-year period, subject, however, to annual parliamentary approval and any terms and conditions that may be attached. The agreement is valid initially for a six year period but may be extended by mutual consent.

Recently, Canada has introduced a new type of federal-provincial partnership agreement that was first signed between Canada and Ontario in November 2005, simultaneous to the Canada-Ontario LMDA. The partnership agreement was created fill a major gap by making programmes available to the uninsured unemployed (women immigrants, young people) since regular active programmes under the Labour Market Development Agreements are primarily focused on providing services to persons on unemployment insurance.

Regionalisation is another model of political decentralisation. Several previously highly centralised political-administrative systems have devolved power to strong regional governments, including major responsibilities in the field of labour market and employment policy (*e.g.* Belgium, Italy and Spain, Poland).

Prior to the decentralisation reforms Spanish employment policy was primarily a responsibility of the central state, managed and implemented by the Public Employment Service (*Instituto Nacional de Empleo*, INEM). INEM was exclusively responsible for the core functions of labour market policy: placement services, active policies, including training and employment promotion, management and payment of unemployment benefits. Now, as a consequence of the decentralisation process, the autonomous communities and local authorities implement active policies related to employment and training, within the framework established by the national administration. Basic labour legislation, including labour market regulations and the social protection system, remain a national responsibility. Regional governments apply labour legislation and develop active policies adapted to their own needs. The regional authorities are also responsible for local economic development. INEM remains exclusively responsible for the administration of unemployment benefits. Initially, the management of vocational training was transferred and, beginning in 1996, other active policies. As of 2004, 16 of the 17 Spanish "Autonomous Communities" had established their own employment services.

Although the governments of the autonomous communities have a certain flexibility, they are required to spend the funds they receive for active policies for specified purposes (*i.e.* training, or employment for people with disabilities) and in accord with the applicable state regulations for these programmes. National funds for activite employment policies are allocated to the Autonomous Communities in six programme funding blocks, and there is at present only limited discretion to shift funds between programmes. There are a series of basic principles to which the regional employment services must adhere (Ruiz, 2003).

In Poland regionalisation reforms in the previously highly centralised state administration have led to a corresponding decentralisation of responsibility for the formulation and implementation of labour market policies to the 16 new regional and 339 county self-governments (Table 4.1).

Table 4.1. **Levels of Polish government and PES after the administrative reform**

National labour office	
1: Ministry of Labour and Social Policy	● Co-ordinates the activities of public employment service (PES).
	● Develops major programmes.
	● Manages labour fund.
	● Ensures uniform application of law.
Regional labour offices(16)	
2(a): Regional state administration (voivod)	● Oversight of compliance with national law and regulations by PES at regional and county levels.
2(b): Regional self- government (marshal)	● Prepares and implements the Regional Plan of Activities in Support of Employment.
	● Analysis of regional labour market.
	● ESF administration.
County labour offices (339)	
3: Local county (poviat) self-government (Staroste)	● Prepares and implements the local programme in support of employment.
	● Job counselling and placement.
	● Implements active policies.
	● Benefit administration.
	● Local labour market monitoring and analysis.

Source: Ostrowska, 2008.

Municipalisation of service delivery is a third model of political decentralisation. This is found especially in the organisation of labour market services for social assistance recipients, which in many countries is primarily the responsibility of the local authorities. This type of decentralisation is practiced, for example, for the new German Basic Income Support for Jobseekers in Germany as well as for social assistance clients in the Netherlands.

The German Basic Income Support for Jobseekers, which came into effect in January 2005 (Hartz IV), provides a new framework for integrated provision of benefits and labour market services to the long-term unemployed and other employable social assistance recipients. Under the new legislation all needy unemployed persons not eligible for the regular Unemployment insurance Benefit (SGB III) are eligible for the new Unemployment Benefit II (SGB II), a consolidated benefit near the social assistance level, which is funded by the federal government and administered jointly by the PES and the municipal authorities. New joint agencies (*Arbeitsgemeinschaften*) or Jobcenters are responsible for providing not only the new unemployment benefit II but also for active programmes to all employable social assistance beneficiaries, including social services provided by the local authorities. The final legislation also permitted 69 local authorities (municipalities and counties) to assume full responsibility for placement and active programmes as well as for benefit administration. The legislation defines this local option as a limited experiment for a period of 6 years until 2010. In 353 local districts so-called joint agencies or Jobcenters in which there is co-location and close co-operation between local social agencies and the PES were established.

In this case, the Jobcentre is established on the basis of a contract agreement between the local authority and the local PES. There is a clear division of labour in the Jobcentre between the PES and the local authorities. The PES is responsible for the financing and implementing active measures and for the administration of Unemployment Benefit II. The social agency of the local authority is responsible for the administration and financing of rent subsidies and traditional social services (*e.g.* debt, drug and psychological counselling, child care). In the experimental municipalities the local authority is fully responsible for providing all services for this client group.

Accountability problems in Germany have arisen especially in connection with the municipal option. For example, it has proven extremely difficult to establish a common data base between the PES-led Jobcentres and the 69 local option counties and municipalities because of differences in IT systems and in data standards in implementing agreed common indicators. Moreover, the responsible (BMAS – the Federal Ministry of Work and Social Affairs) has only limited supervisory authority over them because they are subject to the jurisdiction of the *Länder* (state) governments. For example they are not included in performance management system of the ministry, which even faces constitutional limitations in exercising finance controlling over their activities that it funds.

In a comparable experiment in Denmark the municipalities are now solely responsible for the delivery of employment services to all client groups in 14 pilot job centres. In the pilot job centres the municipal council alone approves the performance audit and the employment plan. By 1st August 2009 all job centres will be run by the municipalities. However, in the unitary state administration in Denmark the delegation of operative responsibility takes place within the context of a strong national system of performance standards supervised by the regional labour market authorities (Box 4.2).

Box 4.2. **Minimum requirements for municipal employment plans and Danish national performance targets**

1. At a minimum the job centre employment plan must include:

   ● The targets set by the Minister of Employment.

   ● Description of the most important future employment policy challenges based on the national targets, the performance audit, and the analysis undertaken by the Employment region and the Employment council.

   ● Local strategy and targets for the employment efforts.

   ● Strategy and targets for the service provided by the job centre to enterprises.

   ● Strategy and targets for the involvement of external actors in employment activities.

   ● Budget for employment activities apportioned between the municipality and the state.

2. The Danish Minister of Employment set the following three targets for 2008:

   Performance target 1: The job centres need to ensure a decrease in the number of unemployed people over 3 months.

   Performance target 2: The job centres particularly need to focus on people who have been unemployed for more than a year, as well as the targets set under the national initiative known as "A New Chance For Everyone".

   Performance target 3: The job centres need to ensure a decrease in the number of unemployed young people (those under 30).

3. "New Chance for Everyone" targets.

   This initiative was introduced to enable those receiving social security and starting allowance (a reduced benefit rate for refugees and immigrants) to support themselves and to participate in employment or training to a greater extent. The two-year national targets are that:

   1. 25% of the target group will enter employment or training.

   2. The target group will be self-supporting 15% of the time.

   3. The target group will be participating in an activation scheme 40% of the time.

Source: Hendeliowitz, 2008.

Elements of decentralisation and flexibility: What can be decentralised?

It is useful to define more precisely what decentralisation or flexibility could mean in the context of public organisations and service provision. The elements listed here represent an initial stocktaking of basic elements of flexibility in implementation. They are drawn in particular from my own experience in analysing labour market policies but are in principal also applicable to organisations in other policy areas. Ideally, we would want to answer some such set of questions in order to assess the degree of decentralisation or flexibility in labour market policy (or other policy areas) in a given national setting.

Goals and performance management

- To what extent are organisational goals and targets centrally determined or do they allow room for sub-national (regional and local) goals and hence flexibility in adapting goals to local circumstances and local strategies?

- Are targets and indicators hierarchically imposed or bargained with regional and local actors?

- Is performance assessment based solely on quantitative criteria or integrated in a process of dialogue that takes local conditions and strategies into consideration?

- Are sanctions imposed or is the MBO process largely a consultative framework?

Organisation of service delivery

- Is the organisation of service delivery centrally regulated or are local operating units of the PES and other service providers relatively free to adapt organisational structures for service delivery to local actor constellations and conditions? Here there is a certain argument for standardisation in the management and controlling of organisations at the national or regional level but also for flexibility in adapting them to local circumstances.

- Software and data systems are central to modern PES organisations and structure to a very large extent processes and the interaction with clients. To what extent is standardised software and IT systems used or are local operating units free to use their own software and IT systems? Local software may increases process flexibility at the expense of standardised data collection and transparency in assessing performance at the national level.

Integration strategies

- Are local actors free to determine the programme mix and even adapt design features of programmes, including target groups, or are these largely centrally determined? May local PES offices implement innovative programmes outside the standard programme portfolio? There may be a trade-off between local flexibility and equality of service provision in the national territory.

Financing

- Are the resources available to regional and local operating unit adequate? Transfer of responsibilities to regional and local authorities must be accompanied by adequate financial resources to carry out the assigned tasks.

- Do regional and local actors have flexible global budgets or line item budgets for active measures? Can funding not used in one year be carried over into the next fiscal year? A key element in administrative or political decentralisation is whether regional and local operating levels are free to allocate resources flexibly between budget items for active measures. In traditional line item budgets flexibility for operating units is low.

Personnel

- To what extent are local organisational units free to hire, recruit, train and pay personnel and to assign them to tasks at their own discretion, subject to the usual limitations of collective agreements and the public service?

- Is the budget for administration and personnel costs centrally determined and inflexible or interchangeable with programme expenditures? For example, are operating units free to decide what services to contract out to external providers?

Accountability

Different meanings

Four principal types of accountability criteria can be identified, which central authorities are typically concerned to uphold even in decentralised systems (Mosley, 2003):

- Legal accountability: Public agencies are expected to act on the basis of the rule of law and in conformity with applicable regulations.

- Fiscal accountability: Correctness and economy in the use of public monies. Public bureaucracies are expected to minimise costs and account for expenditure based on law.

- Performance accountability: Output-oriented effectiveness and efficiency: whether declared goals have been achieved and whether the results justify the resources committed.

● Public accountability: Democratic public administration requires political accountability to elected government officials but also responsiveness to the needs and preferences of citizens (*e.g.* the Citizens Charter in the United Kingdom).

In more traditional systems of public administration, the accountability framework emphasises legal and fiscal accountability and the separation of administration and politics, whereas "new public management" gives greater emphasis to decentralisation, managerial discretion, performance measures, quality standards and consumerism in accountability frameworks.

Accountability standards may conflict. For example, a strict interpretation of legal and fiscal accountability may be an obstacle to increased discretion of managers at the operative level to promote improved performance, for example, when reporting requirements for programmes or expenditures are too onerous. Participation of the social partners or local actors in decision-making may be inimical to managerial efficiency, for instance, if there is a lack of agreement on goals or if there is a conflict of interest, *e.g.* when local actors are themselves service providers.

Trade-offs between decentralisation and accountability

Experience with decentralisation in its different forms suggests a number of typical or trade-offs between decentralisation and accountability.

Overriding national policy objectives

Labour market policy is in most countries a national priority that requires national co-ordination. For example, in Sweden classical active labour market policy was regarded as a "national and integrated component of economic policy and thus a pre-eminent national concern" (Behrenz *et al.*, 2001). In countries with high wage replacement rates (*e.g.* "flexicurity" in Denmark) ALMP and robust activation polices are part of the national system and cannot be entirely left to local discretion. Even Switzerland has in recent years moved toward a more co-ordinated and directed labour market policy with a strong evaluation system in place for regional PES offices (Hilbert, 2006). The national importance and the financial volume of expenditure for labour market policy in most countries place limits on the degree of decentralisation that is politically acceptable. The question in most countries is rather what degree and what types of decentralisation are desirable and feasible within the framework of national policy.

Interest conflicts

Conflict of interest between local actors implementing active labour market policy (ALMP) and national interests represented by central authorities is an important justification for central rules and regulations in labour market policy. For example, programmes that subsidise local firms may distort competition and merely lead to job loss elsewhere in the country. Unregulated this could lead to a "'prisoners' dilemma game entailing long-run losses for all" (Behrenz *et al.*, 2001). Subsidised employment may displace regular employment. From a national perspective labour mobility to different parts of the country may be preferable to the lock-in effect of local training or job creation programmes. In a Swedish study PES managers were sceptical about giving more control over ALMP to the municipalities and concerned about the municipal representatives' alleged lack of knowledge and understanding of the aims and functioning of ALMP measures and "local protectionism and municipal rent-seeking" (Behrenz *et al.*, 2001).

Moreover, the design of the financing system for labour market policy may have important consequences for efficiency and effectiveness. If local expenditures are not tied to local revenue generation bureaucratic rent seeking may be encouraged in delivery systems in which implementation is devolved to lower levels of government "since vertical fiscal transfers may allow local officials to ignore the financial consequences of mismanagement" (Fisman and Gatti, 2002). Insofar as local actors are required to bear an appropriate share of the costs of funding programmes the agency problem inherent in decentralised administration can be mitigated.

Performance accountability

Decentralised systems, especially those with forms of political decentralisation, frequently face major problems due to the variety of organisational forms and lower level of standardisation and comparability in labour market and performance data. Insofar as different jurisdictions enjoy flexibility in programme design their performance at the programme level is *per se* difficult to compare, especially since flexibility can also mean differences in data collection requirements. Moreover, different regional and local jurisdictions frequently use different software, which further compounds the problem of collecting and exchanging standardised performance data.

The accountability framework of the Workforce Investment Act in the United States can be regarded as an attempt to adapt performance management to the special tasks and problems of multi-level governance. It establishes a common performance accountability framework for programmes implemented by state, and local governments and private sector partners. There is a small set of core performance indicators for different target groups, while state and local governments are free to include additional indicators beyond these minimum requirements. Importantly, the core indicators (*e.g.* entering employment; retention after 6 months; earnings) are largely gathered at low cost from unemployment insurance wage records. Formal performance agreements with the states establish performance targets and provide in principal for sanctions. In this complex and decentralised system there have been formidable problems both in developing comprehensive data and information systems and in reconciling differences in the definition of core indicators (*e.g.* job placement). The accountability framework is also a major concern in current debates in the US over reform of the Workforce Investment Act. State and local officials frequently criticise federal regulations and accountability requirements for limiting flexibility and impeding adaptation of programmes to local needs (Eberts, 2003; Dorrer, 2003).

Spain and Canada have experienced similar accountability problems due to the difficulties of establishing a common information system and data exchange for the multi-level governance system. In Spain, in the course of decentralisation, some regions had opted for their own information systems with different data bases and software. In the process of agreeing common definitions of a number of basic concepts (claims, job offers, duration of unemployment, job matching, etc.) administrative practices as well as information systems had to be adapted to ensure compatibility (Ruiz, 2003; Rymes, 2003).

In the case of political decentralisation, flexibility in programmes and service delivery models needs to be reconciled with the need for a national policy framework. This usually requires a legislative framework or co-ordinating mechanism, the development of a common set of performance indicators and a system for the exchange of labour market data, and minimum standards of service for citizens throughout the national territory. In Canada and the United States this takes place on the basis of negotiated labour market development agreements with the provinces or performance agreements with the states. The leverage of central authorities over independent state or provincial governments is based in particular on central funding. In principal the US Department of Labor can suspend payments to US states that fail to fulfil their obligations under the applicable performance agreement, although this does not happen in practice. In regionalised systems, in which the central government has more legislative powers, co-ordinating bodies are established. For example, in Spain the national Minister for Labour and Social Affairs and the representatives of the ministries of the Autonomous Communities meet in the Sectoral Conference for Labour Affairs to resolve conflicts and insure a common national framework.

Legal accountability

In this sense conformity with the law and applicable regulations and fiscal accountability, *i.e.* correctness and economy in the use of public monies, remains an important criteria for success in decentralised systems. Insofar as decentralisation entails the devolution of legal and financial supervision and controlling to lower tiers of government the unintended effect is as a rule different level of oversight and different interpretations of the relevant regulations in different jurisdictions.

Finally, it should be noted that accountability frameworks impose substantial costs for keeping and auditing financial and administrative records, programme monitoring and evaluation and contract management on organisations. These costs would appear to increase with the complexity of the delivery system and the number of actors of different types involved.

Local flexibility

What decentralisation actually means in terms of the transfer of responsibility to local levels of government or administration[2] can vary, depending on whether flexibility in the provision of employment services at the sub-national (state, province, regional) level is actually passed on to local actors. Four dimensions are particularly important for local praxis: resource flexibility, programme flexibility, eligibility criteria and performance goals.[3]

Budget flexibility

Flexibility in the allocation of budget and personnel resources is an essential prerequisite of local PES flexibility in labour market policy. A few countries allocate funds for active measures in the form of block grants that can be flexibly allocated by local PES actors. In many countries there is some freedom to shift funds between budgets lines. However in others, local actors appear to have little or no budget flexibility. The reasons why traditional line items budgets for active measures are still retained in some countries are not entirely clear. Presumably it is a product of the strength of traditional notions of accountability as fiscal accountability and commitment to central control. International experience suggests that budget flexibility can be conceded to local PES actors without posing serious accountability problems. Accountability should be secured by focusing on output or performance rather than on inputs and by normal accounting practices rather than by line item budgets.

The German case is interesting in that it combines budget flexibility with room for central initiatives. There is a global "reintegration budget" for active measures for SGB III (insurance) programmes in the 178 local employment agencies, who decide on the allocation of their funds to various programmes. National priorities are imposed through the planning of targets in the MBO system (outputs) rather than through control of inputs in the form of line item budgets. On the other hand, the government makes additional funds available for special programmes of high priority that are earmarked for specific purposes, for example, the "Initiative 50 plus" for the older unemployed. This division of labour has the advantage of retaining flexibility in local PES budget allocations, while at the same time giving the government the possibility of intervening on high priority issues on an *ad hoc* basis. Local PES agencies are free to apply for these funds for special programmes or not at their own discretion.

Programme flexibility

The degree of flexibility that local/sub-regional employment agencies have in the design and mix of their programme portfolio (labour market training, job creation measures, employment subsidies, etc.) varies markedly across OECD countries. In most countries that practice administrative decentralisation (MBO) or allocate funds in the form of block grants to sub-national authorities, local administrators can choose their own programme mix from the centrally determined programme menu. In a few countries (*e.g.* Switzerland) local actors have considerable leeway in designing programmes specifically to meet local needs, within broad national guidelines. In other countries only a limited share of local funding is available for innovative programmes not foreseen in the national guidelines. For example, in Germany and Austria, 10% of budget for active measures can be used freely for innovative programmes. In many countries, however, local PES actors appear to have little or no flexibility with regard to programme mix or programme design. International experience suggests, however, that at minimum local actors can be given considerable leeway in shaping their local programme mix and be allowed to allocate a portion of their resources to innovative programmes not foreseen in the national programme portfolio.

Eligibility criteria

In most countries decisions on eligibility for programmes and the allocation of services to specific target groups are made at the national level and relatively inflexible for local actors (OECD, 2007a). In Germany, for example, there are as a rule legally mandated eligibility requirements based typically on duration of unemployment. Only where programme eligibility requirements are non restrictive, *e.g.* unemployed persons, do placement staff have discretion. In addition to eligibility requirements mandated by law, so-called "action programmes" prescribe what types of services the unemployed are to receive based on a profiling system that classifies clients according to their distance to the labour market and service needs. Management systems of this sort are used to standardise processes and increase management control over resource allocation in local service offices.

A principal reason why eligibility criteria are centrally determined is that policy makers in most countries have a strong propensity to articulate policies and define their public initiatives with reference to target groups (youth, women, long-term unemployed, older workers, etc.). In many cases, performance targets are also defined in terms of labour market target groups. The reasons for this pattern are clear: Labour market policies serve not only the unemployed but also to maintain public support for governments. The political accountability of elected officials appears to override considerations of local flexibility. Indeed, a recurring argument for centralism in policy management is the need for national officials to articulate and implement national policy initiatives in a timely fashion in response to their perception of national needs.

Performance management

In performance management systems national PES operational targets need to be realistic but also "stretching" in that they stimulate local actors to enhance their performance under given local labour market conditions. Typically these targets are estimated for the coming year at the national level on the basis of labour market projections and past performance and then disaggregated to the regional and local level in a complex negotiation process. The negotiation process is necessary in order to come to realistic targets for local PES units but also to foster commitment on the part of local actors to organisational goals. The extent to which this process is hierarchical or consensual varies greatly across countries. Whereas negotiations play a strong role in many countries, even those with national PES organisations that practice administrative decentralisation, in a large number of countries local actors appear to have little or no flexibility in the determination of local performance targets. However some MBO systems explicitly include local targets (e.g. Austria, Germany), which is an important component of flexibility for local actors.

The degree of flexibility in a performance management system also depends on the type of targets that are centrally set. For example, during the crisis of the 1990s in Sweden ALMP central goals came to be defined in terms of the number of participants in labour market measures instead of broader labour market goals as had been the case in the past. This type of target reduces the amount of local policy discretion as the local PES is told what to do rather than which labour market goals are to be achieved by its own choice of means (Behrenz *et al.*, 2001).

Decentralisation and local policy co-ordination

Decentralisation and the degree of flexibility actors have in implementing policy is also important from the perspective of local co-ordination of labour market and employment policy. Responsibility for employment services is itself frequently dispersed. In many OECD countries (*e.g.* Belgium, Denmark, Finland, Ireland, the Netherlands, Portugal, Sweden, Switzerland) job brokerage and responsibility for active programmes are concentrated within the PES and benefit administration is the responsibility of separate agencies. In other countries (*e.g.* France) responsibility for placement services and active measures are assigned to two or more separate institutions. In a few countries (*e.g.* Germany and Austria) the national PES provides a full range of integrated employment services. In federal systems with devolution of substantial responsibilities to provincial or state governments there is an even more complicated division of labour (*e.g.* Canada and the United States). Finally, in many countries services for the unemployed on social assistance are provided in a separate delivery system in which local authorities play a major role (*e.g.* Denmark, the Netherlands, Germany). Great Britain is one of the few countries that concentrate responsibility for all labour market services for all client groups in one national agency, the Jobcentre Plus network, which merged responsibility for welfare to work programmes for social assistance recipients with PES services for other unemployed.

Beyond employment services, policy implementation also requires co-ordination between relevant actors in related policy domains (*e.g.* local economic development, educations and training and social policy). This means that decentralisation in, for example, the public employment service cannot be introduced without considering the necessary linkages with local actors.

Initial findings from ongoing OECD studies suggest strongly that the degree of decentralisation or flexibility local actors enjoy is of crucial importance in forging joint local strategies (OECD, 2009). Local policy actors are as a rule embedded in national or regional administrative and accountability structures that constrain their room for manoeuvre in adopting and implementing joint strategies at the local level. For example, if local employment services, education or economic development agencies institutions have little discretion in allocating their funds or adapting their programmes and schedules they will not be able to work effectively in implementing local skill strategies (OECD, 2007b, OECD, 2007c).

In Korea the improvement of policy co-ordination at the local level is a principal focus of regional policy (Box 4.3). Since 2005, regional employment councils, local employment supporting networks and local employment and human resource development (HRD) programmes have been established to better link actors at different levels of government and in related policy areas (*e.g.* industrial, welfare and employment).

Capacity building at the regional and local level

Decentralisation of responsibility for labour market and employment policies presupposes that local actors dispose of the requisite capabilities. These include being able to co-ordinate local actors; analyse local needs, develop appropriate strategies, implement programmes, monitor, control and evaluate performance, and comply with the accountability standards that may be required by higher level authorities.

Box 4.3. **Korean regional policies**

1. Strengthening local governance and network:

   - Establishment of Regional Employment Councils (REC) chaired by governor.

   - Local Employment Supporting Networks (LESN) composed of various agencies related to employment service.

   - New regional employment teams at the Ministry of Labour headquarters and in job centres.

2. Introduction of local programmes to enhance job creation and HRD (2006):

   - Through projects such as experts network and LMP to meet the needs of local industries and research activities.

   - With participants from local labour and business groups, universities and NGOs.

   - By financial support given up to KRW 300 million per project, following annual assessment (for up to three years).

   - 135 projects are funded within the total amount of KRW 9 500 million in 2007.

3. Promotion of decentralisation and co-operation:

   - Some LM programmes have been decentralised to local job centres, including job search assistance and career guidance programmes (2006), training programmes for the unemployed (2007).

   - Co-operative relationships built between job centres and local governments, for example, many events such as Job Fairs are jointly organised.

   - National job information network (named Work-net) is connected to local authorities and can be accessed through their homepages.

Source: Lee Jae-Kap, 2008.

The concept of capacity building, which is widely used in the context of development politics, has been criticised for being a chameleon-like concept without precise meaning (Harrow, 2001). In our view capacity building remains a useful concept in organisational studies despite the proliferation of meanings. Decentralisation policies need to take into consideration and be adapted to the capabilities of regional (or state or provincial) and local authorities.

The relevant capabilities depend on the actual policy responsibilities delegated or devolved to sub-national levels in a particular institutional setting and on the specific local deficits. In general, internal capacity building requirements within decentralised state structures can be summarised in terms of (Ohiorhenuan and Wunker, 1995):

● Personnel capabilities: technical, managerial, and administrative skills need to carry out the assigned tasks in a professional manner.

● Organisational capabilities: governance and management structures, IT systems, standardised procedures and processes, accountability structures.

● Fiscal capabilities: Resources need to be appropriate to responsibility. Sub-national actors have to be equipped with the necessary resources to carry out the tasks assigned to them and have sufficient flexibility in the allocation of these resources between programmes to meet local needs.[4]

Local capacities also depend on the scale of local administrative units. For example, decentralisation of the public sector in Denmark was accompanied by a consolidation of smaller administrative units deemed too small to carry out the tasks given (Hendeliowitz, 2008).

When responsibilities for labour market services are decentralised, there will be in most cases a need for support services for local actors. There is also a strong need to assist local leaders by providing labour market expertise and technical analytical capacities. Other likely needs are, for example, for the provision of IT services and labour market data, internal training for employees, recommendations and consulting services on work process organisation, programme guidelines or model programmes, audit and accounting services, legal advice and counselling. These supportive services can be provided in various ways by regional or national authorities or by local partners who dispose of the required resources and expertise, for example, the local public employment service. Regional and local authorities also need to develop their own technical expertise, managerial, and administrative skills and organisational capacities to meet new tasks, either internally or by contracting for services through external providers. Local capacity building efforts in Korea include the establishment of regional co-operation teams and regional labour market analysis teams in job centres and local expert networks on employment and HRD (Lee Jae-Kap, 2008).

In Germany, the development of state consulting firms to support the implementation of regional labour market policies is an innovative example of regional capacity building (Box 4.4). The importance of labour market policy in Germany's 16 *Länder* (federal states) increased greatly since the 1990s as a consequence of the regionalisation strategy funded by the structural funds of the European Union. To cope with their new responsibilities most of the states created new intermediary organisations to assist the traditional ministries and support regional and local actors involved in of implementing labour market policy. These consulting companies and service providers perform a

---

Box 4.4. **Functions of German state sponsored consulting firms for regional capacity building**

- Internal consulting services for the state ministry in matters of:
  - Programme development or direct development of programme proposals for state labour market policy.
  - Reform of the state's policy and funding instruments.
  - The selection of providers of labour market or industrial policy programmes and projects.
- Co-ordination of the co-operation between the state ministries, regional PES agencies, and other local labour market policy actors; development and maintenance of Internet-aided project databanks.
- External consulting services and support – substantive and legal counsel, including assistance with grant application, for example local actors planning or conducting projects, providers of further training, outplacement companies, businesses, business start-ups and individuals.
- Internal research and communication, expert reports, and organisation of public hearings as well as external publications and public relations.
- Continuous monitoring of the labour market, internal controlling and evaluation of programmes, including budgets and expenditure.
- Programme administration tasks: independent administration and disbursement of project funds and, in some cases, all ESF funding.

Source: Mosley and Bouché, 2008.

---

primarily advisory and co-ordinating function in the practical implementation of an integrated regional policy (Mosley and Bouché, 2008).

Finally, regional and local authorities can vary greatly in their administrative and technical capacities and in their political will to assume responsibility for particular tasks in the design and delivery of employment services. This is a strong argument for some degree of flexibility in decentralisation from the national to the regional/state level or to local authorities for which asymmetrical decentralisation of employment services in Canada or the local option in Germany are interesting examples.

Conclusion

A few conclusions emerge from the preceding analysis:

- Within the field of labour market policy the movement toward decentralisation has been concentrated in particular in the area of active labour market policies, whereas benefit systems remain centrally regulated and, with some exceptions, centrally administered.

- It is important to distinguish between policies and implementation. Even in countries with relatively decentralised delivery systems there is usually a strong effort to retain an overall common policy framework, accountability standards and co-ordinating mechanisms for active programmes.

- We can observe two major types of PES decentralisation in OECD countries: administrative decentralisation, especially in PES organisations with MBO-type systems, and political decentralisation. The former represents a form of organisational flexibility that is basically a managerial strategy. In practice one can observe two clearly different MBO-types: the more centralised and hierarchical agency model and the more decentralised self-administration model.

- Political decentralisation, or devolution, may entail not only managerial discretion but usually a more far-reaching delegation of responsibility for policy implementation from the national to the sub-national (regional, state, or municipal) levels of government.

- Decentralisation may enhance policy delivery by adapting it to local circumstances but may also have unintended negative effects, for example, uneven quality in service delivery or accountability problems related to the fragmentation of responsibility, especially where different tiers of government are involved, and lack of comparable performance data. There is thus a strong argument for minimum quality standards and standardisation of managerial information systems in decentralised regimes.

- Four principal types of accountability can be identified: i) legal accountability; ii) fiscal accountability; iii) performance accountability; and iv) public or political accountability. These perspectives may in practice entail goal conflicts. For example, a strict interpretation of legal and fiscal accountability may be an obstacle to increased discretion of managers at the operative level to promote improved performance, if reporting requirements for programmes are too onerous.

- Accountability standards are themselves costly and need to be reasonable. They impose substantial costs for keeping and auditing financial and administrative records, programme monitoring and evaluation on organisations. These costs appear to increase with the degree of decentralisation and the ensuing complexity of the delivery system and the number of actors of different types involved.

- Experience with decentralisation in its different forms suggests a number of typical or trade-offs between decentralisation and accountability: First, labour market policy is in most countries a national priority that requires national co-ordination. Its perceived importance and the financial volume of expenditure for labour market policy place limits on the degree of flexibility for regional or local actors that is politically acceptable. Second, potential conflicts of interest between local ALMP actors and national interests are an important justification for central rules and regulations in labour market policy. For example, programmes that subsidise local firms may distort competition and merely lead to job loss elsewhere in the country. Third, decentralised systems, especially those with forms of political decentralisation, frequently face major problems in performance accountability due in particular to the number of organisations involved and the lack of standardisation in labour market and performance data available.

- What decentralisation actually means in terms of the transfer of responsibility to local levels of government or administration can vary, depending on whether flexibility in the provision of employment services at the sub-national (state, province, or regional) level is actually passed on to local actors.

- Local flexibility in OECD countries in the four dimensions considered is uneven. Budget flexibility in the form of block grants in contrast to line item budgets is an important element of local flexibility that is not available in many countries. International experience suggests that budget flexibility can be conceded to local PES actors without posing serious accountability problems. Accountability can be secured by focusing on output or performance rather than on controlling financial inputs through line item budgets. In many countries, local PES actors have little or no flexibility with regard to programme mix or programme design. International experience also suggests, however, that at minimum local actors can be given considerable leeway in shaping their local programme mix and be allowed to allocate a portion of their resources to innovative programmes not foreseen in the national programme portfolio. The extent to which MBO-type managerial systems are hierarchical or negotiated varies greatly across countries. The negotiation process is necessary in order to come to realistic targets for local PES units but also to foster commitment on the part of local actors to organisational goals. Some MBO systems explicitly include local targets, which is an important component of flexibility for local actors.

- Local policy actors are as a rule embedded in national or regional administrative and accountability structures that constrain their room for manoeuvre in adopting and implementing joint approaches at the local level. The degree of flexibility local actors enjoy is thus of crucial importance for co-operative local labour market strategies.

- Decentralisation of responsibility for labour market and employment policies presupposes that local actors dispose of the requisite capabilities. Because regional and local authorities may, at least initially, lack the experience and organisational capabilities required for assuming a larger role, decentralisation needs to go hand in hand with capacity building.

Notes

1. As in other cases of devolution, there are particular problems with the integrity and comparability of performance data exchanged across multiple governmental levels (Rymes, 2003).

2. What decentralisation and flexibility at the "local" level actually mean is unclear, given the large differences in the size of countries and the various tiers of multi-level governance to which authority may be transferred (national, state or regional, provincial or county, PES agency of municipal level).

3. See OECD, 2007a, for recent international survey of these issues in OECD countries.

4. The number of municipalities was reduced from 271 to 98 and the counties were replaced by five new administrative regions.

Bibliography

Behrenz, L., L. Delander and H. Niklasson (2001), "Towards Intensified Local Level Co-operation in the Design and Implementation of Labour Market Policies: An Evaluation of some Swedish Experiments and Reforms", in J. de Koning and H. Mosley (eds.), *Labour Market Policy and Unemployment: Impact and Process Evaluations in Selected European Countries,* Edward Elgar, Aldershot, pp. 256-290.

Davies, A.C.L. (2001), *Accountability. A Public Law Analysis of Government by Contract,* Oxford University Press, New York.

Dorrer, J. (2003), "The US: Managing Different Levels of Accountability", *Managing Decentralisation. A New Role for Labour Market Policy*, OECD Publishing, Paris.

De Vries, M. (2000), "The Rise and Fall of Decentralisation: A Comparative analysis of Arguments and Practices in European Countries", in *European Journal of Political Research,* Vol. 38, No. 2, pp. 193-224.

Straits, R. (2003), "The US: Decentralisation from the Bottom Up", *Managing Decentralisation. A New Role for Labour Market Policy*, OECD Publishing, Paris.

Fisman, R. and R. Gatti (2002), "Decentralisation and Corruption: Evidence Across Countries"*Journal of Public Economics*, No. 83, pp. 325–345.

Harrow, J. (2001), "Capacity Building as a Public Management Goal", *Public Management Review*, Vol. 3, No. 2, pp. 209-230.

Hendeliowitz, J. (2008), "Making Labour Market Policy More Flexible While Preserving Accountability", presentation at the *OECD Conference on Decentralisation and Co-ordination: The Twin Challenges of Labour Market Policy*, Venice, 17-19 April 2008.

Hilbert, C. (2006), "Ein anreizkompatibles Kontrollinstrument der regionalen Arbeitsvermittlung: das Modell Schweiz und dessen Potenzial für die Bundesrepublik" (*Incentive-Control Instruments in Regional Employment – The Model of Switzerland and its Potential for the Federal Republic*), in G. Schmid, M. Gangl and P. Kupka (eds.) (2004), *Arbeitsmarktpolitik und Strukturwandel: Empirische Analysen. Beiträge zur Arbeitsmarkt – und Berufsforschung,* No. 286. IAB, Nurnberg, pp. 133-152.

Jackson, K. (2008), "Making Labour Market Policy More Flexible While Preserving Accountability – Canadian Perspectives", presentation at the OECD Conference on Decentralisation and Co-ordination: The Twin Challenges of Labour Market Policy, Venice, 17-19 April 2008.

Lee, J.K. (2008), "Initiatives for Local Employment Policy in Korea", presentation at the OECD Conference on Decentralisation and Co-ordination: The Twin Challenges of Labour Market Policy, Venice, 17-19 April 2008.

Mosley, H. (2003), "Flexibility and Accountability in Labour Market Policy: A Synthesis", Managing Decentralisation. A New Role for Labour Market Policy, OECD Publishing, Paris.

Mosley, H. (2005), "Job-Centres for Local Employment Promotion in Germany", in S. Giguère and Y. Higuchi (2005), Local Governance for Promoting Employment, Institute for Labour Policy and Training, Tokyo, pp. 165-178.

Mosley, H. and E. Sol (2005), "Contractualism in Employment Services: A Socio-Economic Perspective", in E. Sol and M. Westerveld (eds) (2005), Contractualism in Employment Services. A New Form of Welfare State Governance, Kluwer Law International, The Hague, pp. 1-20.

Mosley, H. and P. Bouché (2008), "Germany: The Local Impact of Labour Market Reforms", in S. Giguère (ed.) (2008), More Than Just Jobs: Workforce Development in a Skills-based Economy, OECD Publishing, Paris.

Mosley, H. and K.U. Müller (2007), "Benchmarking Employment Services in Germany", in J. Dekoning (ed.) (2007), Evaluating Active Labour Market Policy: Measures, Public-Private Partnership and Benchmarking, Edward Elgar, Cheltenham, pp. 275-308.

Mosley, H. and E. Sol (2001), "Process Evaluation of Active Labour Market Policies and Implementation Regimes", in J. de Koning and H. Mosley (eds.) (2001), Labour Market Policy and Unemployment: Impact and Process Evaluations in Selected European Countries, Edward Elgar, Aldershot.

Mosley, H., H. Schütz and N. Breyer (2001), "Management by Objectives in European Public Employment Services", Discussion Paper FS I 01-020, Social Science Research Centre (WZB), Berlin.

OECD (2009 forthcoming), Breaking Out of Silos: Joining up Policy Locally, OECD Publishing, Paris.

OECD (2007a), "Decentralisation and Co-ordination: The Twin Challenges of Labour Market Policy", Preliminary background note for the 2nd Vienna Conference, November, OECD Publishing, Paris.

OECD (2007b), "Integrating Employment, Skills and Economic Development (IESED)", Progress Report, OECD Publishing, Paris.

OECD (2007c), "Designing Local Skills Strategies", Interim Report, November 2007, OECD Publishing, Paris.

OECD (2003), Managing Decentralisation: A New Role for Labour Market Policy, OECD Publishing, Paris.

OECD (1999a), Decentralising Employment Policy – New Trends and Challenges, OECD Publishing, Paris.

OECD (1999b), "Managing Accountability in Intergovernmental Partnerships", OECD Publishing, Paris.

Osborne, D. and T. Gaebler (1992), *Reinventing Government. How the Entrepreneurial Spirit is Transforming the Public Sector*, Addisson-Wesley, Reeding, Massachusetts.

Ohiorhenuan, J. and S. Wunkler (1995). "Capacity Building Requirements for Global Environmental Protection", *Global Environment Facility (GEF) Working Paper No. 12*, Washington DC.

Ostrowska, C. (2008), "Making Labour Market Policy More Flexible While Preserving Accountability", presentation at the OECD *Conference on Decentralisation and Co-ordination: The Twin Challenges of Labour Market Policy*, Venice, 17-19 April 2008.

Prud'homme, R. (1995), "The Dangers of Decentralisation", *The World Bank Research Observer*, Vol. 10, No. 2 (August), pp. 201-20.

Ranson, S. and J. Stuart (1994), *Management for the Public Domain*, MacMillan, Basingstoke.

Richards, S. (1994), "Devolving Public Management, Centralising Public Policy", *Oxford Review of Economic Policy*, 10 (3): 40-50.

Rhodes, R.A.W. (1981), *Control and Power in Central-local Government Relations*, Gower, Aldershot.

Ruiz, D. (2003), "Spain: Modernisation through Regionalisation", *Managing Decentralisation. A New Role for Labour Market Policy*, OECD Publishing, Paris.

Rymes, D. (2003), "Partnerships Across Levels", *Managing Decentralisation. A New Role for Labour Market Policy*, OECD Publishing, Paris.

Lundin, M. and P. Skedinger (2006), "Decentralisation of Active Labour Market Policy: The Case of Swedish Local Employment Service Committees", *Journal of Public Economics* (90), pp. 775-798.

Tanzi, V. (1996), "Fiscal Federalism and Efficiency: A Review of Some Efficiency and Macroeconomic Aspects", in M. Bruno and B. Pleskovic (eds.) (1996), *Proceedings of Annual World Bank Conference on Development Economics 1995*, World Bank, Washington DC.

Tiebout, C. (1956), "A Pure Theory of Local Expenditure", *Journal of Political Economy*, 64, pp. 416–424.

Simonin, B. (2003), "France: Providing Greater Flexibility at Local Level", *Managing Decentralisation. A New Role for Labour Market Policy*, OECD Publishing, Paris.

Sol, E. and M. Westerfeld (eds) (2005), *Contractualism in Employment Services*, Amsterdam University Press, Amsterdam.

ISBN 978-92-64-05918-4
Flexible Policy for More and Better Jobs
© OECD 2009

Chapter 5

The Role of Labour Market Policy in Horizontal Co-ordination

by

Randal W. Eberts

Successful co-ordination of workforce development and economic development programmes can help local areas better compete in a global economy by responding more effectively to the needs of workers and businesses, encouraging more innovative practices and entrepreneurship, promoting social cohesion, leveraging government resources by partnering with non-government organisations, and instilling more local ownership in local decision-making and strategic initiatives. However, the potential of horizontal co-ordination among local agencies and organisations has not yet been fully realised. More than a simple restructuring of government, rather it requires a cultural transformation among management, staff, and policy makers. This means greater attention to customers, the balance between accountability and flexibility, appropriate mechanisms and incentives, performance-based monitoring, strategic planning and goal setting, alignment, strong leadership, and trust among partners.

Introduction

The question posed in this chapter is how can decentralisation of government be associated with a higher degree of horizontal co-ordination of workforce development and economic development activities. As competition in the global economy intensifies, countries increasingly realise that their future economic success rests with building a more flexible and knowledgeable workforce. Within the global context, the ability for local communities to create and retain good jobs depends more upon their ability to compete in terms of product quality and customer service than on costs. To do so, their workforce must possess the appropriate skills, engagement and motivation and meet the immediate and future needs of employers.

It is widely understood that to meet these challenges workforce development and economic development policies and activities must be better co-ordinated horizontally at the local level, which includes the ability to forge wide-ranging partnerships among government and non-government entities. Many countries have been moving toward a more decentralised approach of providing workforce development and economic development services. Since the 1980s, governments have sought to devolve responsibilities from central government agencies to lower tiered governments or to push administrative responsibilities from central agencies to local offices. They see decentralisation as a way to move decision-making closer to workers and businesses so that they can respond more effectively to their needs. Empowering local agencies and organisations also creates an environment of innovation and experimentation to better understand how best to serve their customers and to provide a platform by which to integrate the array of services targeted at the multiple challenges of workers and businesses. In addition, forming partnerships with local non-government agencies provides a means to leverage public funds with community resources.

The move toward decentralisation and horizontal co-ordination is also driven by broader forces affecting government. These include pressures for government to be more accountable to citizens, increasing expectations of citizens to participate in decision making and growing recognition by governments of the need to engage with citizens in solving problems. These lead to a more customer-centric approach to providing services and thus structuring government.

Yet, despite efforts by an increasing number of countries, many contend that decentralisation has not led to the desired outcomes expected from horizontal co-ordination and integration of government services. Participants of the first Venice Conference on Decentralisation held in 1998 concluded that focusing on decentralisation alone would not accomplish the desired goals (OECD, 1999). Decentralisation is considered a necessary condition for local actors to work together on the complex and cross-cutting issues that affect their ability to serve the needs of individual workers and businesses. But there are many other conditions that must be met before decentralisation can lead to successful horizontal co-ordination.

Giguère (2008) aptly states the challenges of co-ordinating government services with particular attention to workforce development and economic development efforts:

> The governance of employment and skills is complex. Neither decentralisation nor partnerships appear to provide sufficient answers to the harmonisation of national and local objectives. Overall, the problems of human resource development have not been satisfactorily addressed through the transfer of powers to regions; and co-ordination of policies cannot be forced at local level. The main reason for this seems to be that the strict performance requirements associated with the management of public programmes at local level by and large reflect national policy goals. Therefore, a key challenge for the future will be the provision of greater flexibility in the management of policies so that they can be better adapted to local circumstance and co-ordinated with other initiatives if needed, while maintaining full accountability and maximum efficiency in service delivery. Secondly, stronger strategic capacity is required at local level to link up programmes, initiatives and local stakeholders.

As underscored in the statement, key issues that must be addressed in order to bring about horizontal co-ordination of government services include harmonising objectives within the vertical government structure and striking the proper balance between flexibility and accountability within the framework of decentralisation and horizontal co-ordination.

Studies of government initiatives that promote decentralisation and horizontal co-ordination point to more basic issues. At the core of these recommendations is the realisation that successful co-ordination requires not simply rearranging government organisational structures but rather effecting change in behaviour and the culture of government agencies and other partnering organisations. This requires that all aspects of government – governance, legal, finance, business rules, and technical procedures – be examined and brought together into a coherent arrangement. The most effective structural arrangement is a network of agencies and partners in which authority and responsibility are distributed among the various participants. Establishing a viable network requires a strong focus on: leadership, strategic planning, customer focus, information and analysis, human resource development, and performance results. Since networks are linked together by a commonly held vision and shared goals and objectives, strong leadership emerges as one of the critical ingredients. Leaders must define the common purpose of the network, educate partners on the importance of cutting across the respective boundaries of their organisations that may separate their efforts, and continually hold partners accountable for their performance.

The purpose of this chapter is to identify elements that are critical in achieving horizontal co-ordination of government services. Initially, it is established that workforce development and economic development initiatives are local issues that require local decision-making and administration of services. The structure by which workforce development and economic development activities are organised is described, by first highlighting initiatives pursued by selected countries to integrate workforce programmes and to co-ordinate workforce and economic development services. Then the chapter briefly reviews the reform movements initiated in the 1980s to decentralise government services, pointing out the deficiencies of focusing only on structural changes and not on behavioural and cultural changes within the agencies. Lessons learned from these initiatives are summarised by listing ten key areas that well-functioning organisations should focus on, and issues related to co-ordinating workforce development and economic development programmes are discussed. Finally, the chapter concludes by pointing out that criteria gleaned from government reform are similar to those pursued in best practice businesses in the private sector.

Workforce development and economic development: A local issue in a global economy

The delivery of employment and training services to workers and the provision of economic development assistance to businesses are local issues. Workers and businesses interact within a local labour market and the needs of workers and businesses are to a large extent determined by the conditions and characteristics of local labour markets. These markets typically vary with respect to industrial composition and worker skills, and a one-size-fits-all approach to national policies is typically not appropriate for framing and meeting the needs of workers and businesses. Furthermore, increased globalisation has placed greater emphasis on local markets and has blurred the lines between national ones. This not only has important ramifications for addressing these issues locally instead of nationally but it also offers lessons from the private sector with respect to the importance of networks in delivering services.

The global economy is rapidly transforming into a myriad of networks of enterprises that transcend national boundaries. In most instances, they are linked more closely to local industrial clusters than they are to the confines of national borders. Thus, as the world moves more toward a landscape without borders, the role of nation states as producers of goods and services is being replaced by networks of industrial clusters as the predominant economic entities. Furthermore, globalisation of trade creates pressure to harmonise a wide variety of laws and policies across regions within nations. It also puts pressure on national governments to equalise the different economic situations across regions that result from global networks favouring one industrial cluster over another. Public workforce development and economic development organisations increasingly recognise that the old paradigm of centralised decision making and service delivery makes it more difficult to serve the needs of workers and businesses that are competing within this global arrangement.

In response to the forces of globalisation, private enterprises are increasingly moving to a network form of organisational structure. According to an ILO report on global production and local jobs, "the development of transnational networks of economic activities generates unprecedented possibilities for accessing new markets and resources, acquiring new skills and capabilities, and developing international competitive advantage" (ILO, 1998). The shift by firms to a network form of organisational structure leads to a decentralisation of decision making and a greater reliance on horizontal co-ordination across functions and units. Co-ordination takes place among affiliates of multinational corporations, among different business functions such as R&D, design, production, and marketing, as well as within individual units or functions. Decentralisation of decision-making across these vertical and horizontal networks allows firms to be more responsive to external changes. Being part of a network allows individual units to focus on their core business while taking advantage of the collective size of the overall network. This provides economies of scale, scope, and integration while avoiding the costs and rigidities of vertical integration.

The ILO report highlights characteristics that are seen to promote the success of the global networks, which may provide a new organisational model for local institutions and actors involved in both workforce and economic development policies:

- Large firms are moving away from hierarchically organised, vertically integrated structures to more horizontally co-ordinated structures in order to increase their capacity to innovate, react more quickly to external changes, improve product quality and cut down on operating costs.

- Governance structure plays a key role, and relations among network members must be defined on the basis of shared interests in order for co-operation to develop.

- From a strategic perspective, the co-ordination of global production networks requires some degree of centralisation necessary for an efficient use of resources, a rapidity of decision making, and a global vision to be achieved within the network.

- The network is neither opened for anyone to join nor closed to all new entrants but permeable so that organisations that the network deems essential to its overall goals can be included.

- A lead firm is important to continuously engage in attracting and selecting network members, sustaining network relationships by managing conflict and learning, in positioning the network in the market and in building the structure and the culture of the network.

Governments, while making progress in responding to these ever-changing needs through the restructuring and reorientation of policy, decision making and service delivery, have not yet achieved the full potential of meeting the needs of their customers. Unlike businesses that understand the imperative of changing their culture and capabilities to remain competitive in a global economy, governments often struggle to grasp the essential elements necessary to make the full transformation and are reluctant to shed their previously held ways of doing business and the culture embedded in their traditional government structures. Nonetheless, the evidence is clear that local communities that foster and sustain forward-looking institutions that find new and flexible ways of co-ordinating workforce development and economic development activities can nurture the industrial competitiveness, worker development and social cohesion needed to compete successfully in the global economy.

Provision of workforce and economic development services

During the past few decades, several countries have restructured their workforce development systems and economic development programmes in order to be more responsive to the needs of local businesses and workers. These efforts have produced the workforce development systems and collaborative arrangements that are in place today. The transformation process presents important lessons regarding the critical factors that should be in place in order to improve horizontal co-ordination and thus enhance the local policy impact. Before discussing lessons learned from these initiatives and others, it is useful to describe the workforce development systems and economic development programmes in selected countries in order to provide examples that can be referenced in the later discussion regarding lessons. It is also necessary to provide examples of viable partnerships between workforce development organisations and economic development entities in order to gain a sense of the types of co-ordination across organisations-public and private. This section provides a brief overview of four workforce systems: i) the Workforce Investment Act (WIA) in the US; ii) Jobcentre Plus in the UK; iii) Centrelink in Australia; and iv) the Employment Service in France, and offers examples of economic development initiatives and efforts to co-ordinate workforce and economic activities within those countries and others.

Workforce development programmes

Workforce Investment Act (US)

The United States provides workforce development services through a strong federal-state-local partnership. This federal approach to providing social services was established when the first employment programmes were implemented nearly 75 years ago. More recent programmes, such as the Workforce Investment Act (WIA) of 1998 and the new welfare reform initiative – the Personal Responsibility and Work Opportunity Act of 1996 – have followed the same design but with even more emphasis toward the devolution of authority to state and local government entities.

Under WIA, employment programmes are designed and delivered through a system of workforce boards that exist at the state and local levels. The federal government determines the types of programmes that they will fund, such as training and labour market exchange, the amount of dollars available, the target groups, and the performance goals. State-level workforce boards develop strategies and policies that govern the administration of workforce programmes within their states but within the guidelines of the federal regulations. Local workforce investment boards (numbering more than 600) gather business and community input and try to tailor the programmes to meet their local needs. Funds flow from the federal agencies through the states to the local workforce investment boards. The local boards then subcontract with other government agencies or non-governmental organisations to provide services that are delivered through one-stop service centres. In many states, one-stop centres house services provided through several agencies, including WIA, Wagner-Peyser employment services, and some social service agencies. The local boards negotiate with the state and the states negotiate with the federal organisations on the performance goals for each programme within each programme year.

Centrelink (Australia)

The Australian government created Centrelink about the same time the US enacted WIA. Centrelink is an agency of the Department of Human Services, which was newly created in 2004 in a broader re-organisation that brought together six service delivery agencies under the department's auspices. The stated outcome of Centrelink is to provide access to government services that effectively support self-sufficiency through participation in employment, education, training and the community. Its strategic priorities include delivering services and payments to those workers and families in need, developing the capabilities of Australia's people, and fostering opportunities to collaborate with other agencies. Some of the factors contributing to its ability to forge strategic collaborations are: its service-oriented architecture, information governance, business process management, security management and relationship with key vendors. At the national level, Centrelink is governed by a small executive committee which reports to Centrelink's chief executive officer. Services are provided through 328 customer service centres and 25 call centres.

Jobcentre Plus (UK)

Jobcentre Plus (JCP) is a UK initiative that merges workforce development services with income support. It was established in 2001 with the creation of the Department of Work and Pensions, which merged Employment Services with the Benefits Agency. JCP's mandate is to help more people into paid work, help employers fill their vacancies, and give people of working age the help and support they are entitled to if they cannot work. JCP integrates the payment of three types of benefits (lone parents, sick and disabled, and job seekers allowance) with employment services and job training. The emphasis of JCP in recent years is to encourage work and to provide services that will get people into work. Jobcentre Plus operates a network of around 1 000 integrated offices as well as call centres. The offices function primarily as assessment and referral centres, and the call centres serve payment centres. Jobcentre Plus relies on partners to provide other services to customers. Employment and job training services are subcontracted to other organisations, and Jobcentre Plus works closely with community sector agencies and health professionals to deal with the issues of housing, drug abuse, and poor health.

ANPE (France)

France has until recently followed a highly centralised workforce development system, however new reforms have enabled a more joined up approach to employment policy (Box 5.1). In 1998, a new reform has merged the organisations respectively responsible for active (ANPE) and passive labour market policy (UNEDIC). The reform should have a strong territorial

Box 5.1. **France's territorial dimension of employment policies**

France has traditionally followed a highly centralised workforce development system. The design, implementation and delivery of services were operated by the central government with little variation across territorial governments. Beginning in the early 1980s, with the passage of the decentralisation acts of 1982 and 1983, the central government devolved new powers and responsibilities to local governments. At first, the responsibilities mostly focused on regional economic development, requiring local governments to develop plans, referred to as Concerted Development Pacts. The purpose of the plans is to lay out specific steps to promote development, create and attract new activities while preventing job loss and workers dislocation.

In 1983, France also devolved the management of public policy regarding vocational training to the country's regional authorities. However, division of responsibility for defining and implementing vocational training programmes and policies among state, regional authorities, and professional organisations remained an issue. The regions were given responsibility for the construction, maintenance, and physical operation of vocational school buildings themselves. However, the central government retained control over management of the public service of teaching. Each region established and financed its own regional training programme for continuing vocational education while the central government retained the prerogative for the legislative and regulatory framework of continuing vocational training. The regions were left free to evaluate their needs for and organise apprenticeship programmes. The regional powers first granted in 1983 were reinforced by the passage of a five-year law 1993, making the regions responsible for the training of youth who lack jobs and job skills outside the school system. It also expanded the regions' role as leaders and co-ordinators by establishing a Regional Development Plan for Vocational Training for Young People. During this time, dialogues were initiated at the territorial level among management, unions, and local government agencies to help promote greater co-ordination among these key stakeholders.

In February 2008, the French government passed a law to reform the public employment service by merging the National Employment Agency (ANPE) and the National Union for Employment in Industry and Commerce (UNEDIC), thereby creating a single operator for both the employment service and the administration of unemployment benefits. The new organisation will have six responsibilities:

- Examine the labour market.
- Be the contact point for jobseekers, as well as inform, guide and support them in their job search.

**Box 5.1. France's territorial dimension
of employment policies** *(cont.)*

- Register jobseekers.

- Provide unemployment benefits and welfare benefits *(aide de solidarité)*.

- Collect, process and disseminate data, as well as make these available.

- Help and support jobseekers in co-operation with local authorities.

    The new organisation is faced with not only successfully merging the two organisations into a coherent and effective single operator, but also in developing a workable relationship with territorial and local entities that are carrying out various employment assistance functions, such as vocational training.

Source: Boissard (2008).

---

dimension allowing the various regional entities to define their priorities according to the needs of their local workers and businesses. Yet considerable work still needs to be done to make the employment system truly a territorial one in France. The territorial dimension has to overcome the past dominance of the central government and the many layers of territorial entities in order to integrate workforce development and economic development effectively at the territorial levels. However, there are signs that the two decades of decentralising workforce and economic development activities have paid off for France. Many have attributed the improvement in France's labour market over the past several years in part to the ability of local entities to better assess and respond to the needs of workers and businesses at the territorial level.

Economic development programmes

Government and non-government entities share the responsibility of designing and implementing local responses to economic development needs. In some instances, municipalities and other local government entities, such as counties and states in the US and territorial governments in Europe, assume the sole responsibility for administering certain programmes. Other countries, particularly those with national industrial policies, give their central governments more responsibility for carrying out economic development initiatives. This is particularly true among several European and Asian countries which pursue national policies that target specific industries or industrial clusters for technical and financial assistance. Japan is well-known for its national industrial policy that developed cities around specific industry clusters, such as automobiles or electronics. Italy has pursued an industrial policy for the past 50 years to address the economic disparities between the northern and southern parts of their country. And more recently, European countries, specifically Germany, France and the UK, have collaborated to support an aerospace industry.

In both Europe and the US, partnerships between private and public entities have been formed to pursue economic development efforts. In Europe, the European Union has endorsed and encouraged partnerships, and the number of local economic development agencies has reached more than 500. The Committee of the Region and the Economic and Social Committee both emphasise the importance of adopting a bottom-up perspective that places the needs of citizens and deprived communities at the centre of any new initiative. In the US, which has a tradition of a local decentralised approach to providing government services, local partnerships to promote economic development are the norm. Economic development is primarily the responsibility of state and local governments, with only limited assistance from the federal government. Yet, many federal programmes encourage, if not require, that their programmes go through local partnerships.

Right Place Programme (United States)

At the local level, the Right Place Programme in Grand Rapids, Michigan is an example of an economic development organisation in the US that has successfully partnered with other local agencies. It is a private, non-profit organisation focused on promoting economic growth in the urban core of a metropolitan area with a population of more than a million people. The Right Place provides the standard set of economic development services (*e.g.* information on industrial sites, tax abatements, state wide business incentives) and works closely with businesses to help them connect with the proper government agencies to receive the appropriate incentives and assistance. In addition, it has partnered with other organisations to offer several unique programmes. One such initiative, partnered with the City of Grand Rapids, redevelops abandoned industrial land in the inner city. Such a venture is risky, since companies seeking to locate in an area are more attracted to undeveloped "greenspace" than to urban locations with uncertain payoffs.

Regional Development Agencies (UK)

At a broader regional level, the UK has created Regional Development Agencies (RDAs) in England, the Scottish Enterprise, and the Welsh Development Agency. The RDAs, for example, were established in 1999 to help drive growth in England. Recognising the diverse nature of the English economy, the central government sought to push responsibility for economic development to the local stakeholders. It has granted RDAs flexibility and autonomy to respond to the particular challenges and opportunities of their regions. Recognised as the strategic leaders of economic development and regeneration within their region, RDAs work with local authorities to decide how best to focus their attempts to fulfil their responsibility. Each RDA is responsible for drawing up, in collaboration with local and regional partners in all sectors, a Regional Economic Strategy (RES) for the region. The role of the RES is to provide a shared vision for the development of the region's economy to improve economic performance and enhance the region's competitiveness. Its aim is to ensure that all those responsible for economic development work together to develop common goals and priorities for the region's economic development. A fifteen-member board leads each RDA. The minister of the Department of Business Enterprise and Regulatory Reform appoints the board members, who are senior stakeholders from business, labour organisations, local government, and the voluntary sector.

Regional councils (Finland)

In the mid-1990s, Finland created regional councils that operate as regional development and regional land-use planning authorities (see Box 5.2). Each of the 19 councils is governed by representatives from municipalities within their region, and each is assigned statutory responsibility for regional development in collaboration with state regional authorities. Their creation marked a transfer of focus and control from central government to local authority. The work of the regional councils emphasises long-term planning. The key tasks of the regional council are to create a development strategy for the region, promote the vision incorporated in the strategy and maintain the strategy and to revise it when necessary.

Box 5.2. **Reforms to employment and economic development policy in Finland**

Finland has had a long history of developing and implementing models for decentralising government services from the national to regional and local government and for co-ordinating government services both vertically and horizontally. In 1994, Finland created 19 regional councils that operate as regional development and regional land-use planning authorities. Each regional council is assigned statutory responsibility for regional development in collaboration with state authorities. The council's governing board is comprised of representatives from municipalities within each council's region. Their creation marked a transfer of focus and control from central government to local authority. The delegates on the decision-making bodies of the regional councils are influential political appointees of the member municipalities, which gives the councils the mandate to represent the political will of a region's inhabitants and also reinforces the municipalities' considerable autonomy and responsibility.

Box 5.2. **Reforms to employment and economic development policy in Finland** (*cont.*)

Regional councils emphasise long-term planning. Their key tasks are to create a development strategy for the region, to promote the vision incorporated in the strategy, to maintain it, and to revise it when necessary. More specifically, the council draws up regional development programmes and co-ordinates them with other regional administration authorities, presents objectives for infrastructure development, develops a framework for business activity, and improves the occupational skills of regional residents. In addition to their responsibility for matters internal to their region, regional councils also take care of international relations and affairs connected with European Union regional policy. The councils draw up programmes required for the granting of support from EU structural funds for their own regions and then play a major role in implementing the programmes. The ability to deal independently with international agencies, instead of first going through the Finnish central government, marks a significant level of autonomy of local governments and is consistent with the earlier discussion of the decline in importance of national governments in favour of more regional authority in a global economy. The regional councils are funded primarily by their member municipalities through annual membership fees determined on a per inhabitant basis.

Shortly after the forming the regional councils, Finland created regional Employment and Economic Development Centres that co-ordinate the regional operations of the Ministry of Trade and Industry, the Ministry of Labour and the Ministry of Agriculture and Forestry. Each of the 15 T&E Centres are charged with promoting business, employment, and rural vitality within their regions. More specifically, the Centres provide services to help companies with product development, technology transfer, export assistance, and business development and financing. They also help entrepreneurs start and nurture their own businesses. For workers, T&E Centres provide an employment exchange, vocational counselling, training and education, and vocational rehabilitation. Services are generally free, except for some customised services for businesses.

Most recently, Finland's new national government has created a new Ministry of Employment and the Economy, combining the former Ministry of Labour and the Ministry of Trade and Industry and the Regional Development section of the Ministry of the Interior. The reform was more than a way of joining functions and tasks under one administrative entity but of establishing a new ministry that would function as a whole and assume a new vision and culture of co-ordination of services. The stated goal of the new Ministry is to respond with foresight to changes in the global economy and to create the conditions at all levels of government for taking action that will be successful in the network economy. The new Ministry creates the opportunity to invest in companies' innovations and productivity and to develop and ensure the availability of a well-trained labour force.

Source: Cronberg (2008).

Regional development strategies (France)

Until the 1980s, France followed a centuries-old tradition of a centralised approach to economic development. However, passage of the decentralisation acts of 1982 and 1983 granted local governments new powers and responsibilities to develop plans (Concerted Development Pacts) for regional economic development and to implement those plans. A law passed in 2004 further refined the role of local governments in devising these plans (Greffe, 2008). It requires regions to devise a plan that lays out specific steps to promote development, create and attract new activities, while preventing job loss and dislocation (Greffe, 2008). The plans are to take into account a region's strengths and weaknesses by analyzing their economic competitiveness and identifying competencies both with respect to their industries and their workforce. Most recently, regions are expected to establish linkages among companies, research centres, training institutions, and other stakeholders (Greffe, 2008). Once a plan is properly vetted through the regional political process, the regional and central governments negotiate the amount of funding that will be available to implement the plan.

Initiatives that integrate workforce development and economic development efforts

This section offers examples of efforts to integrate and co-ordinate workforce development and economic development activities. These examples are chosen to illustrate the approaches typically taken and to contrast co-ordination efforts at the central *versus* local government levels.

Regional Workforce Preparation and Economic Development Act (California)

An example of an initiative that promotes horizontal co-ordination of workforce development and economic development programmes is California's Regional Workforce Preparation and Economic Development Act (RWPEDA) of 1998. Faced with a growing concern that the state's workforce development system was not responding to emerging workforce education and training needs, the state legislature took the initiative and passed the Act. At the time, it was a unique effort designed to bring education, workforce preparation, and economic development partners together at the state and regional levels. The goal was to create an integrated, effective and responsive workforce development system that would better meet the needs of employers and jobseekers and improve the quality of life for all Californians.

In its attempt to integrate education, workforce development and economic development programmes and activities, RWPEDA formed partnerships at both the state and local levels. The act had three components.

First, it directed the four state agencies with responsibilities for public K-12 education, community colleges, workforce development and economic development to enter into a memorandum of understanding (MOU) and develop a unified workforce development strategy for the state. To ensure effective implementation of RWPEDA and the MOU a Joint Management Team (JMT) was formed, consisting of executive staff from each of the four agencies. Second, the act instructed the four state-level partner agencies to select and fund at least five regional collaboratives to participate in economic development strategies, and to deliver services to clients in a more responsive, integrated and effective manner. The JMT, operating under the MOU, funded a total of six pilot regional collaboratives. Each pilot developed its own unique strategy for addressing the needs within its region and for implementing regional economic development strategies. Third, the act required the partner agencies to create an integrated state workforce development plan. This plan was to guide the development of an integrated workforce development system at the state and local levels. The JMT developed a policy framework document by soliciting input from a 37-member advisory group.

The RWPEDA legislation supported the creation of locally initiated regional collaboratives in order to bring together workforce development partners to test strategies for integrating and improving both service delivery and workforce development systems at the regional level. Six regional collaboratives were awarded funding. They represented a diverse range of geographic, economic, and proposed programme characteristics, including single and multiple county regions, rural and urban areas, industrial and agricultural economies, and direct service and system-based activities.

One of the six regional partnerships is the Los Angeles County Workforce Preparation and Economic Development Collaborative. It encompasses Los Angeles County, which is home to 10 million people and stretches across a large geographic area. It is served by multiple community college districts, K-12 public school districts and workforce development entities – including eight separate Workforce Investment Boards – and also includes enormous county agencies that manage the CalWORKs and employment programmes. Despite being a large county with multiple stakeholders and wide-ranging needs and interests, the collaborating partners succeeded in developing countywide projects to support employers and jobseekers, according to the evaluation. Some of the activities initiated by RWPEDA have been sustained beyond the project period; this was made possible by securing additional funding as well as securing the continuing interest and support of the partners.

A distinguishing feature of the California initiative is the leadership at the state level. The legislation brought together the four key government agencies through a memorandum of understanding and the creation of a joint management team that included the top officials of each department.

Co-ordination at the top was seen as necessary in order to have co-ordination at the local levels.

Workforce Innovation in Regional Economic Development (US)

A somewhat contrasting initiative is Workforce Innovation in Regional Economic Development (WIRED), initiated recently by the US Department of Labor (Box 5.3). Similar to the California RWPEDA, this programme was created

---

Box 5.3. Workforce Innovation in Regional Economic Development (WIRED)

Recognising the increasing challenge of global competition on the viability of regional economies, the US Department of Labor initiated a programme that helps regions develop a workforce and mobilise their existing assets to compete more successfully in today's global economy. Secretary of Labor Elaine L. Chao announced the first generation of WIRED regions in February 2006. An acronym for Workforce Innovation in Regional Economic Development, WIRED is based on the premise that national competitiveness and regional prosperity are possible if communities learn how to link their various workforce and educational institutions with regional businesses and innovation assets to ensure that new and emerging industries have the knowledge resources needed to grow and prosper. The US Department of Labor's Employment and Training Administration (ETA) selected 13 regions through a competitive process. Each of these first generation WIRED regions receive approximately USD 5 million per year for three years as well as access to ongoing technical assistance. Since then, 26 additional regions have been selected as second and third generation WIRED regions, receiving similar levels of financial support from ETA.

The WIRED regions are required to focus attention on four key factors shaping innovation and human capital development:

1. The importance of science, technology, engineering, and math competency in new and emerging products and industries.

2. An increased recognition that innovation is critical to global competitiveness.

3. Close interaction and co-operation among regionally based industrial, research, education, and commercialising institutions as a way to mobilise and leverage regional assets.

4. An emphasis on development talent through integrating workforce development and educational institutions with innovators and entrepreneurs.

118

Box 5.3. **Workforce Innovation in Regional Economic Development (WIRED)** *(cont.)*

Each of the 13 Generation I WIRED regions selected specific target industries as engines for economic growth. The most prominent industries were: 1) advanced manufacturing; 2) bio-fuels; 3) life sciences, health sciences, and agricultural science; and 4) information technology applications, software and telecommunications. To support the needs of their targeted industries and to promote the transformation of their regional economy, the WIRED regions have engaged in activities. These include asset mapping to benchmark a region's needs and assets; support and development of entrepreneurship; ensuring that an ongoing supply of workers is recruited and prepared to fill the needs of employers in the region; workforce training targeted at incumbent, displaced, or dislocated adult workers; innovation and technology transfer; and leadership development.

Although an interim evaluation of Generation I WIRED regions has been completed, there are few quantitative outcomes to gauge the success of the initiative. However, the evaluation cites examples of regions bringing together funding from different separate WIA funding sources to cover the cost of workforce development, bringing new flexibility to better direct resources to meet specific needs, forming regional workforce investment boards that are beginning to think outside their own borders, and the alignment of local workforce investment areas with their regional economic development entities.

Source: Early Implementation of Generation I of the Workforce Innovation in Regional Economic Development (WIRED) Initiative: 2007 Interim Evaluation Report, ETA *Occasional Papers*, Office of Policy Development and Research, June 2008; and Chao (2008).

---

to encourage effective partnerships among local businesses, workforce development, economic development and educational institutions. The ultimate goal of WIRED is to expand employment and advancement opportunities for workers and catalyse the creation of high-skill and high-wage opportunities. Given that one of the significant goals for WIRED is to fully align the public workforce investments with a regional economic growth agenda, WIBs are integral to the programme's success. They are encouraged to work with the state governor's office on the application process and on implementation of the WIRED initiative. Regional partnership teams must include a senior representative of the workforce investment system within the region as the lead, or co-lead, with at least one other regional partner, for the region's WIRED grant activities.

A major difference between RWPEDA and WIRED is that for WIRED only one of the three key federal agencies was involved in its creation – the

US Department of Labor. The Department of Education and the Department of Commerce are absent from the collaboration, or have little involvement. Therefore, local partnership agencies may find it difficult to co-ordinate activities if and when their collaboration runs counter to the regulations and performance expectations of the federal agencies that have oversight over and provide funding for many of the workforce, education, and economic development activities.

The US Department of Labor has initiated three phases, or generations, of WIRED regions. The first generation was chosen in 2005 and USD 15 million was awarded to each of 13 regions over a three-year period. The regions were competitively selected based upon several criteria, including the strength of the partnerships in transforming their regions to meet the challenges of a global, knowledge-based economy. Selection of second and third generation WIRED regions is based on similar criteria, but unlike the first generation, the local WIB must be involved in the initial application and be central in carrying out the strategic plan. The second and third general WIRED regions receive only a third of the funds that the first generation region received from the US Department of Labor. Awards to all three generations of WIRED regions are intended to act as seed funding, catalysing the investment of money from other public and private sources in support of the region's strategy.

Each WIRED region is expected to follow a six-step conceptual framework.

1. Define the regional economy by identifying the surrounding communities that share common characteristics, looking beyond traditional political boundaries.

2. Create a leadership group that represents the major assets of a region and provides a forum for regional economic decision-making.

3. Conduct a regional assessment to fully map the area's assets and identify the strengths, weaknesses, opportunities and risks based on those assets.

4. Develop an economic vision based on those strengths and assets and gain support for that vision from the broad-based regional partnership.

5. Build a strategy and corresponding implementation plan that identifies specific goals and tasks and provides a blueprint for how to achieve the region's economic vision.

6. Identify resources – both to support the region's plan and invest in the region's economy – from a wide range of sources including foundations, angel and venture capital networks, and federal, state and local governments (WIRED Fact Sheet, USDOL, ETA Web site).

The preliminary results of an evaluation of the first generation of WIRED regions have been completed, but the evaluation focuses on process and does not compare the progress of WIRED regions with counterfactual regions. An evaluation of the second and third generations is underway.

Vancouver Agreement (Canada)

The Canadian experience offers another example of co-ordinating services around issues located in a specific area. Announced in 2000, the Vancouver Agreement (VA) brought together central government agencies and other organisations to tackle the problem of urban poverty and decay in the City of Vancouver, British Columbia. Involving 12 federal departments, three provincial departments, and several city agencies, it is regarded as a prime example of effective horizontal management within and between governments. The initiative started with lengthy discussions between the three governments and consultations with the public. The agreement was targeted primarily toward the Vancouver Downtown Eastside, an area where the issues of substance abuse, child poverty, crime, and homelessness ran rampant.

Underpinning the VA was a strategy with three components: community health and safety; economic and social development; and community capacity building. To co-ordinate the activities of the several departments and agencies in meeting these three objectives, an administrative structure was put in place consisting of a policy committee, a management committee and a set of processes designed to engage the community directly in setting priorities and determining the implementation of strategies and action plans. Membership on these committees was reserved for the highest ranking officials from each of the organisations. Below these committees was a co-ordinating team with a small staff. This team helped to staff the 14 task groups, each of which targets its efforts to specific issues addressed by the initiative. The co-ordinating team and tasks do most of the work. The other committees meet far less frequently and see their jobs as developing the overall strategies and priorities and setting out an action plan. Implementation is in the hands of the co-ordinating team.

Regional Partnership Programme (New Zealand)

New Zealand's central government has implemented a Regional Partnership Programme, which seeks to help the country's 26 regions promote sustainable economic development opportunities by responding to local needs. The government provides up to NZD 100 000 to help facilitate the formation of regional partnerships, and the local partnering organisations are expected to contribute 25% of the total central government funding. Organisations within the partnerships include the central government, local economic development organisations, businesses, communities, and the indigenous population (Iwi/Maori) representatives. Workforce development agencies were not included, at least at the beginning of the programme. The local partnerships are required to develop a regional economic development strategy and begin to build the capacity to implement their strategies. The Waikato Innovation Park, which opened in 2004, is one example of partnerships stemming from this government initiative. It is designed to commercialise the research activities at Waikato University and several government-sponsored research institutes located in the area.

Employment and Economic Development Centres (Finland)

In the mid-1990s, Finland created regional Employment and Economic Development Centres (T&E Centres) that co-ordinated the regional operations of the Ministry of Trade and Industry, the Ministry of Labour and the Ministry of Agriculture and Forestry (Box 5.2). Each of the 15 T&E Centres are charged with promoting business, employment, and rural vitality within their regions. More specifically, the centres provide services to help companies with product development, technology transfer, export assistance, and business development and financing. They also help entrepreneurs start and nurture their own businesses. For workers, T&E Centres provide an employment exchange, vocational counselling, training and education, and vocational rehabilitation. Services are generally free, except for some customised services for businesses.

Lessons from decentralisation and horizontal co-ordination reform initiatives

From the previous section, it is evident that efforts to promote the formation of local partnerships to co-ordinate and enhance the delivery of workforce development and economic development services are prevalent in several countries. These efforts and the more general government reform efforts have yielded important lessons for encouraging and improving horizontal co-ordination. This section extracts ten critical areas that need to be addressed in order to achieve successful outcomes. The ten areas are compiled from studies of the reform efforts and from experiences with reorganised workforce systems. Some of the current reform efforts go beyond attempts to co-ordinate workforce and economic development programmes and encompass a broader range of government services. Lessons from these more comprehensive reform movements are nevertheless pertinent for finding ways to enhance labour market policy. Aspects of the workforce systems and economic development initiatives described in the previous chapter will be used to help illustrate the relevance of the ten elements identified as crucial for successful co-ordination.

Many of the reform efforts have been driven by the new public management (NPM) model, most often associated with Osborne and Gaebler

(1992). The movement was based on the premise that putting more responsibility for service delivery into the hands of entities closer to customers and subjecting them to market pressures will lead to more responsive and efficient service delivery systems. The primary focus was to separate policy development from service delivery through privatisation, outsourcing and contracting out, which resulted in the decentralisation of government responsibilities.

Governments have followed two approaches of decentralisation. One is referred to as administrative decentralisation and the other as devolution. Administrative decentralisation occurs within the traditional hierarchical structure in which the central government agency grants some discretion to its regional or local offices in implementing policy and designing programmes. Devolution, on the other hand, involves the sharing of authority to design and implement policies with regional governments. The central government usually remains responsible for the broad policy framework and a large share of the funding; the regional government is granted authority to design programmes and administer the delivery of services according to their perception of the needs of local workers and businesses as long as they stay within the broader national policy framework. By granting local governments more authority to carry out their own policy and devise their own delivery platforms, devolution offers opportunities for co-ordination with other government entities and non-government organisation.

However, decentralisation has not resulted in the level of horizontal co-ordination that many anticipated. Rather, the result in many cases has been a fragmented and compartmentalised government (Giguère, 2008; Ling, 2002). A report by the Australian government on how to improve co-ordination concluded that there is plenty of evidence that decentralisation improved efficiency as agencies took advantage of devolution to align their staffing, administrative resources and assets to the objectives that government has set for them. However, the report goes on to say that "devolution of authority to agency heads and a clear vertical accountability for agency outcomes may make collaboration across organisational boundaries more difficult" (Commonwealth of Australia Management Advisory Committee, 2004).

A subsequent study of Australian government co-ordination efforts asserts that:

> One of the principal barriers to successful co-ordination is the assumption that better use of traditional government systems and processes will result in joined up solutions. Traditional systems and processes are designed to deliver government services from centrally controlled, vertically organised agencies. These systems and processes become increasingly inappropriate as government agencies move away from

traditionally organised service delivery towards more customer-centric joined up approach. (Johnson, 2005)

Consequently decentralisation, simply as a means of devolving responsibilities to another tier of government or of outsourcing services to non-government organisations, lacks the mechanisms and incentives to promote horizontal co-ordination. Therefore, it appears that a new government structure and indeed a new culture are necessary to achieve the desired results of horizontal co-ordination.

Several countries have gone beyond the pursuit of decentralisation alone and have undertaken more extensive reform initiatives to promote greater horizontal co-ordination among government agencies and non-government organisations. Various terms have been used to describe these reforms. They are associated to some extent with specific government reforms, which are given as examples in parentheses. These terms include: "joined-up government" (UK), "connected government" (Australia), "policy coherence," "networked government" (Canada), and "whole of government." Definitions of these terms are not precise, as governments use them in various ways.

Several themes run through these reform efforts that are relevant for understanding how horizontal co-ordination can be better achieved. These lessons apply to efforts to co-ordinate workforce development and economic development programmes, as well as the co-ordination of other government programmes. Key elements gleaned from these efforts include structure, authority and responsibility, balancing flexibility and accountability, shared vision and objectives, leadership, strategic planning and problem solving, performance measures, mechanisms of interaction, and skilled and talented staff.

Structure

The whole-of-government approach to horizontal co-ordination stresses the need to move away from the traditional hierarchical, command and control government systems to one of networks of government agencies and non-government organisations. An Australia report asserted that "true decentralisation implies a sharing of responsibility for decision-making at the local level among a number of actors." However, as previously mentioned, change in structure to a more decentralised form of government brought with it problems of fragmentation, duplication, and compartmentalisation. Consequently, a more focused attempt at co-ordination was required.

A 2004 study released by the Canada School of Public Service defined horizontal co-ordination as:

The co-ordination and management of a set of activities between two or more organisational units, where the units in question do not have hierarchical control over each other and where the aim is to generate outcomes that cannot be achieved by units working in isolation. The structures and processes used to achieve co-ordination can range from informal networks to jointly managed secretariats.

The nature of a network is defined by the distribution of authority among the various organisations within the network. If authority rests entirely with the central government, then the network reverts to a hierarchical, top-down organisation in which the agencies below the top take commands from the central office and have little power to make their own decisions. If authority is shared with lower levels of government, then the network follows a more bottom-up approach. The government agencies may still be under the guidance and policy directives of a central government but they have authority to exercise their discretion on various matters. The decentralisation efforts have attempted to move authority to lower levels of government using a combination of each approach.

The top-down and bottom-up approaches are based on different premises about which level of government is in a better position to serve its citizens. The top-down approach presumes that the centre has the knowledge about what is best for the country (either through its political bodies or through the professionalism and expertise of the staff) and that the centre can devise and impose tools that will foster integration and facilitate the achievement of the centre's objectives (Stoker, 2003). Therefore, a top-down model vests the key policy development and accountability with the centre. It resembles the traditional command and control hierarchical structure.

The bottom-up model gives prominence to community leadership through elected local and regional governments working alongside local stakeholders. It starts from "the premise that many players have different experiences and capacities and as such have something of value to bring to the table of public policy and implementation" (Commonwealth of Australia Management Advisory Committee, 2004). Under a bottom-up approach, the local governments take primary responsible for most policy making and strategic planning and the central governments provide direction on coherent policy across regions and provide funding through a grant-in-aid arrangement.

The concept of networked government and co-ordination among the various entities recognises that no one has all the knowledge and resources or controls all the levers to bring about sustainable solutions to complex issues. Obviously, the question is not which one of the two approaches to follow, but to what extent does government exercise shared responsibilities. From the perspective of co-ordinating workforce and economic development programmes, a network structure that is based upon a bottom-up approach of sharing responsibility for decision making at the local level among a number of actors is well suited to meet the needs of workers and businesses at the local level.

A network with shared responsibilities has two dimensions of relationships. One is the vertical dimension that links the central government with the lower level entities. The other involves the horizontal co-ordination across entities. Co-ordination can occur at the local level as well as at higher levels of government.

The workforce development system in the United States illustrates these two dimensions of partnerships. As shown in Figure 5.1, the first is a vertical dimension linking the different levels of government, from federal to state to county to local workforce investment boards (WIBs). The federal government provides a large share of the workforce programme funds and federal programmes provide the overarching structure for delivering employment services to workers. The federal government delivers these services through partnerships with state government agencies and local entities, specifically Workforce Investment Boards that have discretion (although with limits) on how the funds are spent.

Figure 5.1. **Vertical and horizontal relationships in the US Workforce System**

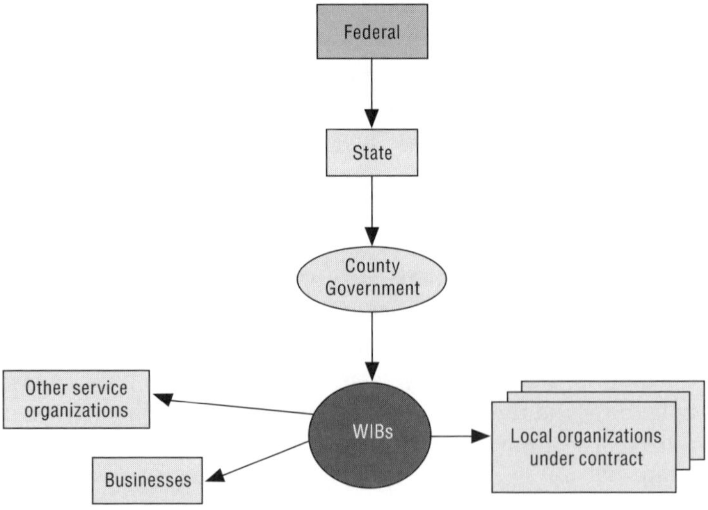

Note: WIBs – Workforce Investment Boards.

The second dimension comprises horizontal partnerships primarily at the local level, in which local workforce investment boards (WIBs) partner with local social service agencies, non-profit organisations within their local jurisdiction, and workforce intermediaries. The WIBs enter into different types of relationships with local entities, creating these horizontal relationships. First, they contract with other government agencies and with non-government organisations to provide the services. Second, they may enter into relationships with social service organisations through memoranda of understanding, which bind them together by explicitly stating that they share a common purpose and serve the same customer base. Third, workforce investment boards may have informal relationships with entities, such as chambers of commerce or non-governmental workforce development agencies, which focus on business retention and recruitment, for example.

Finland's T&E Centres combine services from different Ministries, similar to the US WIA system, but to a broader extent. The US system focuses primarily on services from national workforce development programmes under the auspices of the US Department of Labor. The Finnish system combines workforce development services from the Ministry of Labour with economic development services from the Ministry of Trade and Industry by co-ordinating their functions in each of the 15 Centres across the country. For example, each T&E Centre, in co-operation with the region's employment offices, is responsible for planning, acquiring and monitoring labour market training (adult education as part of the labour market policy), as well as training-related information and development activities. Since both training and economic development services are co-ordinated within one unit, it is possible to match worker training more closely with skill and competency requirements of job openings.

The UK's Jobcentre Plus offers a different configuration of relationships. Jobcentre Plus is a government agency supporting people of working age from welfare to work and helping employers fill their vacancies. Since the Jobcentre Plus offices are extensions of a national department, in this case the Department of Work and Pensions, it does not have the same vertical relationships as the US system. However, Jobcentre Plus does have horizontal relationships, similar to the US system. Jobcentre Plus offices depend upon local partners within their respective districts to provide job training and employment services. Unlike the US WIBs, Jobcentre Plus does not contract directly with these organisations. They originally did, but since last April the contracts have been procured through two other departments. Still, Jobcentre Plus continues to play a key role in the delivery of employment programmes, referring customers to services, representing the national department within local partnership arrangements, and retaining responsibility for local job outcomes and customer satisfaction. Jobcentre Plus also works closely with local authorities, through an Accord with the Local Government Association (similar to a memorandum of understanding), the Learning and Skills Council, and Regional Development Agencies.

Australia's Centrelink provides a third example of relationships within an expanded system of social services. In this case, horizontal relationships are forged not at the local level but primarily at the national level. Centrelink, established by Australia's Parliament in 1997, delivers a range of government payments and services for retirees, families, caregivers, parents, people with disabilities, people who are seeking work or studying, and indigenous people. It also provides wider services at times of major change, such as natural disasters. Although it is an agency under the Department of Human Services, Centrelink delivers these services on behalf of national policy departments and other organisations through a network of 15 districts, and a national call centre. The scope of these services surpasses those offered by WIBs and Jobcentre Plus, which focus primarily on services and payments to workers and the economically disadvantaged. Funding comes from the various departments responsible for these services, most of which are provided through Business Partnership Agreements that join up policy departments and other organisations. Centrelink has also formed strong relationships with other Department of Human Services' agencies during times of emergency response, such as floods, bushfires, and cyclones. It also links state and territorial government agencies in meeting the needs of victims of these disasters. However, there appear to be much fewer horizontal relationships at the local level. In addition, the vertical relationships extend primarily from national departments to their local offices and there are little on-going relationships with sub-national governments.

Another way in which horizontal co-ordination at the lower levels of government can be achieved is by joining together agencies at the top under one department or ministry. By consolidating government functions, they are under one ultimate decision maker – the department's secretary or minister. Both Jobcentre Plus and Centrelink were created from consolidation of government agencies. Canada also followed this approach in creating Human Resources Development Canada in 1993, which was premised on formalising horizontal linkages between departments such as Health and Welfare and the Secretary of State. However, a report on Canada's efforts to achieve horizontal co-ordination concluded that the establishment of a full-fledged agency or department typically involves putting in place a hierarchical structure that is no different from that found in most regular departments, except that it has broader responsibilities and services to meet the needs of its target population. An increase in size creates its own problems of co-ordinating efforts across a larger organisation and in eliciting a sense of ownership among its staff. Moreover, this approach does not avoid the possible lack of co-ordination within an agency and other issues arising from a complex bureaucratic structure.

Another approach is to distribute authority across the various organisations within the network, as illustrated by the US workforce system mentioned above. In this case, the different levels of government assume

128

different responsibilities with the US Department of Labor providing the overall policy directive, the general design of the programme and the administrative of regulations that provide an equitable provision of services to workers across the country. Authority and responsibilities are then assumed by states and local workforce investment boards to administer the policies in ways that best meet the needs of targeted workers and businesses in their locales.

Authority and responsibility

The ability to achieve horizontal co-ordination depends upon governmental units exhibiting sufficient autonomy to respond to local circumstances and to form partnerships with other organisations. If power and authority rests at the central government level, then local entities that are accountable to the central offices may not have the independence to form partnerships or may be conflicted in their relationship with other organisations because of inconsistent expectations.

Federal or decentralised networks of government may be considered bottom-up or top-down, depending upon the authority granted each level of government. Countries, such as Switzerland and the United States, tend toward bottom-up federal systems of government. The Swiss federal system emphasises the sovereignty of sub-central jurisdictions, in which sovereignty is derived from the federal and cantonal constitutions. Both national and local constitutions list the tasks of each governmental level, and they fix the right of governmental entities to levy various types of taxes (Dafflon, 1999). The US has a similar arrangement in which the states have power to tax and provide services and regulate business, which is not explicitly given to the federal government in the US Constitution. Local governments are granted power through the state government.

The relationships among different layers of government can be placed within the framework of fiscal federalism. Fiscal federalism, a multi-layered form of decentralisation, is seen as either competitive or co-operative. In the competitive bargaining model, the various government entities have sufficient authority and resources to enter into mutually beneficial transactions. In this case, each tier of government is given various rights to tax and responsibilities to provide services. They compete with other jurisdictions for households and businesses, which provides a fertile ground for innovation and experimentation, promotes efficiency, and provides a check on the size and scope of government. Governments also compete vertically by positioning themselves for a favourable allocation of resources among the different tiers of government. Power dependence implies that organisations committed to collective action are dependent on other organisations and cannot command the response of each other but rather have to rely on exchanging resources and negotiating common purposes.

The concept of fiscal federalism is based on the premise that specific levels of government are better suited to assume certain government functions than others. Framing the network within the fiscal federalism structure of government forces the following questions:

- Which level of government is closest to understanding the needs of the customers?

- Which level of government is most able to set policy and strategies in dealing with this issue (technical expertise in knowing what works and what does not work)?

- Which level of government is best able to provide funding to support the services provided?

- Which level of government is best able to deliver services most effectively, both directly and with others (co-ordinated services)?

The tension between meeting local needs and meeting national objectives is brought into sharper focus in the context of the global economy. Globalisation stresses the importance of local labour markets over national economies, since industry clusters and one-size-fits-all national policies may not be effective in such a regional environment. But policy at the national level typically emphasises equal rights to citizens and equal access, depending upon the same qualifications (to an extent). It also puts pressure on governments to help compensate residents for disparities in economic fortunes due to the vagaries of the global economy. This can be accomplished through redistribution policy and assistance to distressed areas. Income support, job training, and educational offerings can be targeted to those in a highly economically distressed area. Infrastructure improvements can be provided within the distressed area. Obviously, the redistributive policy and infrastructure improvements should be offered by way of the central government for the purpose of equalising the benefits of global trade across all regions of the country. The central government commonly has the appropriate taxing and budgetary authority and its reach encompasses all regions so that some of its resources can be redistributed from high income, economically vibrant areas, to low income economically distressed areas to mitigate some of the disparities.

Although different levels of government have different competencies in providing workforce development and economic development services, there may be a trade-off between efficiency in providing services and the ability to co-ordinate services if these services are offered by different layers of government. France provides an example of a mismatch between the levels of government responsible for training programmes *versus* those responsible for public employment services. Greffe (2008) points out problems with separating competencies relative to training and labour exchange. The training competence depends upon the central government, since it is controlled by the national Department of Education; the labour exchange services are provided at the municipal level. The lack of co-ordination in policy and implementation between these two key functions in preparing workers for job openings and placing them in jobs may undermine any gains in the efficient provision of these services.

Balancing flexibility and accountability

Within a network structure with shared responsibilities and decision-making, the challenge is to balance flexibility to form horizontal partnerships at the local level with accountability to the higher levels of government. Eggers and Goldsmith (2004), writing on government as networks, reiterates the challenge of accountability:

> The problem of accountability is one of the most difficult challenges of networked government. Without authority and responsibility parcelled out throughout the network, whom do you blame when something goes wrong? How do you achieve results when you have limited control? Ensuring accountability in a networked arrangement is a matter of getting the following four things right: incentives, measurement, trust, and risk. With a good network partner and government manager, the goals and outcomes will stay sharply in focus, but the inputs and processes will change as required.

If a proper balance is not struck, then the network cannot function to its fullest potential in meeting local needs. A network that has too much formal accountability might stop partnerships from responding to citizen needs (Ling, 2002). A network with too little formal accountability may lose its strategic guidance and may undermine the equitable administration of services to individuals in the country for whom the interventions are intended. Moreover, it may lose its political support if legislators and citizens grow concerned about the proper use of public resources.

An Australian report underscores the importance of a balance between the two dimensions of accountability. It suggests that balance can be achieved by encouraging the national level to consult the local level when setting the local targets for labour market policy and vocational training. This would work to ensure that sector performances are compatible with broader area-based strategies, while preserving the integrity of the vertical accountability relationships. But it finds that reconciling (or balancing) flexibility and accountability is the biggest challenge (Commonwealth of Australia Management Advisory Committee, 2004).

An evaluation of the WIA programme in the US came to a similar conclusion that balancing accountability and flexibility under a broad-based federal grant-in-aid programme is critical to success. They added that co-operation among federal, state, and local governments must be maintained on an on-going basis (Barnow and King, 2005).

Jobcentre Plus embraces principles that explicitly state how national priorities and local needs will be weighed. In describing its working relationship with local governments, it declares that "decisions made locally will reflect both the national priorities, local priorities and the views of local communities." It goes on to state that "on financial matters local authorities will have an increase in responsibility and freedom of choice."* What the statement does not say, however, is how well local voices and concerns will be heard by the central office and integrated into policies and the administration of services.

The UK's Regional Development Agencies offer another example of striving to strike an appropriate balance between flexibility and accountability. When creating the Regional Development Agencies, the UK government sought to balance legislated increases in resources, responsibilities and flexibilities to these regions with appropriate accountabilities, incentives and performance management arrangements, while seeking to minimise bureaucracy. In particular, the government commissioned the National Audit Office to carry out an Independent Performance Assessment (IPA) of RDA activity, which aimed to be more transparent, more efficient and less bureaucratic than previous arrangements.

One of the issues, as pointed out by a report issued by the Canada School of Public Service, is that line departments have only limited appreciation of the dual nature of accountability; that is, while there was often a clear sense of what was required within one's own department, the same was not true for broader government responsibilities. They recommend that staff be selected according to their "horizontal co-ordination" skills and that proper training be developed for existing staff.

Shared vision and objectives

An important ingredient in achieving this balance is to establish a shared vision and an agreed upon set of objectives for organisations within the network. While informal networks, which are defined as those that share responsibility among their partners, are best suited to meet local needs, they may lack a clear unifying vision among the diverse group of organisations that make up the network and the lack of strategic control from the central agencies. Partnerships need to establish a shared vision of the customers they serve and the reason for serving them. Since each organisation may come to the network with a different customer base and purpose, it may be difficult to reach agreement on a shared set of objectives.

* Found on *www.jobcentreplus.gov.uk/JCP/Partners/localandnationalpartnerships*.

The ability to construct a shared vision among organisations depends upon the extent to which they share customers. For government departments that provide workforce development and other social services, many of their customers are the same. Jobcentre Plus, for example, recognises that customers face complex problems on a broad array of issues and thus their network of service providers is likely to share a common purpose. In contrast, constructing a shared vision among workforce development and economic development entities may be more difficult. Each has a different customer base. Workforce development programmes serve workers and economic development entities cater to businesses. Whereas labour supply and demand may be considered two sides of the same coin, expectations related to each are not necessarily compatible. Workforce development strives to find work and decent wages for workers; economic development tries to attract business with a quality labour force, but at competitive costs. In addition, the success of many economic development efforts is measured by the number of jobs created, not the wages that they generate.

Culture is also an issue for shaping a shared vision. This is particularly vexing for workforce and economic development entities. Workforce development organisations are accustomed to working with state and federal governments, which require strict accountability, transparent accounting and programmatic practices that are scrutinised closely by funding agencies. Economic development organisations, on the other hand – particularly the non-governmental ones – work behind closed doors in order to strike deals with private business entities.

One of the fundamental responsibilities of the Regional Development Agencies in the UK is to construct a strategic plan that incorporates a shared vision for the development of the region's economy. The same is true for the regional councils in Finland. The strategic planning process aims to ensure that all those responsible for economic development work together to develop common goals and priorities for the region's economic development.

This points to the need for strong leaders who can bring that vision into focus and can hold individual organisations accountable in meeting the agreed upon goals, which is discussed below.

Leadership and trust

Since networks need to be linked together by a commonly held vision and shared goals and objectives, strong leadership emerges as one of the critical ingredients. Leaders must define the common purpose of the network, educate partners on the importance of cutting across the respective boundaries of their organisations that may separate their efforts, and continually hold partners accountable for their performance.

Most contend that government must guide and steer these networks, since they have the authority through the oversight of elected officials and since they provide most of the funds to provide services. As with the private sector model of global supply chains in which a dominant firm must lead, government is the dominant organisation in the network of agencies and non-governmental organisations. Several studies see the central government as playing a key leadership role in networks. A Canadian study (Bakvis and Juillet, 2004) emphasises the role of the central government. It contends that central government should be present at all phases of a horizontal co-ordination initiative and that it should take greater ownership of and responsibility for the results of horizontal initiatives. The study goes on to assert that central agencies need to manage the overall corporate framework, set out appropriate incentives, and create a supportive climate.

Canada's (1996) study "*Managing Horizontal Policy Issues*" further emphasises the importance of central agencies in a network of governments. It contends that central agencies can provide the important impetus for cultural change, which is required to support horizontal issues management. They can influence the approach to interdepartmental co-operation at many levels. They can develop a collegial and collaborative culture across the federal system; they can ensure that the policy process fundamentals are done right; and they can encourage the development of effective collaborative mechanisms.

The Public Services Leadership Consortium, established through the Cabinet Office of the UK central government, brings together a number of the key leadership academies across public services to drive cross-service collaboration and coherence on leadership. The consortium sees leaders as critical for creating a positive environment for reform, creating the right organisational conditions and empowering staff. To promote such leadership and customer focus, the report identified seven key learning areas:

- Understand the spectrum of customer-focused services.
- Assess and analyse who the customers are and what meets their needs.
- Re-align whole organisation systems and processes to deliver better customer focus.
- Enhance the motivation and well-being of staff to deliver excellent customer service.
- Use the local and wider authorising environments to lever and effect change, including methods to empower authority without abdicating responsibility and accountability.
- Set strategic leadership attention to the middle and junior management activities.

● Develop and use entrepreneurial skills of commercial awareness, innovation, and flexibility to procure services across a complex service delivery system.

Of course, strong leadership is also required at the local level. Leaders must bring together the diverse group of organisations through developing a shared vision and agreeing upon performance objectives. They must mobilise resources within the community and within the partnering organisations in order to achieve the desired outcomes. A strong cabinet style executive, given authority through elected representatives, should provide strategic guidance to the diverse committees of local authorities (Chandler, p. 3). For example, Finland's regional councils rely on the political clout of the municipal appointees to mobilise the region around the vision embodied in their strategic plan. Simply following formal procedures or interventions that have been adopted in other areas or that have been prescribed by higher levels of authority may not be sufficient for an effective delivery of services. It may take the abilities of a leader to motivate workers and other partnering organisations to make it all work. The need for strong leadership is particularly important for informal partnerships, in which the relationship is not based on a contract arrangement or a memorandum of understanding, but solely on the shared vision between the organisations.

Partnering organisations must also be advocates for their causes, such as workforce development agencies for workers and economic development agencies for businesses. This advocacy must be ongoing, and organisations must be willing to change their process without changing their goals in order to meet the changing needs and circumstances of their customers. Implementing a programme or set of programmes, which at the time are shown to be effective in serving the needs of workers, does not guarantee that the programme will continue to achieve the same desired outcomes in the same cost-effective manner. The circumstances of workers, the demand for their skills, and general economic conditions affecting the demand for workers with various qualifications, all change over time. Unlike the case with businesses, there is no ongoing market test to indicate the benefit-to-cost ratio of these social programmes.

Leaders of partnering organisations should also be "cheerleaders" for one another, encouraging their organisation to pursue sound procedures and to adhere to rigorous performance goals. Each must recognise that the success of their partners enhances their own performance. With each organisation monitoring the performance of the other partners, a system of mutual accountability can be achieved, in which no central organisation would act as "principal", but rather a community of organisations that hold each other accountable for their actions and progress. However, as previously discussed, many commentators agree that networks cannot be self-governing. Rather, most contend that government must guide and steer these networks, since they have the authority through the oversight of elected officials and since they provide most of the funds to provide services. As with the private sector model of global supply chains in which a dominant firm must lead, government is the dominant organisation in the network of agencies and non-governmental organisations. This makes it even more imperative that government is able to adopt a culture of problem-solving and experimentation, seeking innovative solutions to the needs of customers.

Effective leadership cannot take place without a sufficient level of trust in the leaders and mutual trust among the heads of the partnering organisations. Trust is earned through establishing a process by which partners feel that their input is heard, a common vision is shared, and progress is measured objectively – all the key steps outlined in this section.

Strategic planning and problem solving

Once a shared vision has been established, local partnering organisations need to become problem-solvers. Stoker (2003) contends that for the network structure to be self sustaining it must present a viable solution to a set of problems recognised by policy makers. The first step in this process is to conduct research regarding the needs of the customers and the circumstances that account for such needs. This analysis should be based on accurate and objective information, and the research should be conducted in a rigorous and systematic manner. The next step is to use the information to design a plan that serves the customers. The plan needs input and then endorsement from all parties in the partnership. It also needs to lay out explicit steps that attract, satisfy and retain partnering organisations. Proper metrics should be identified to track the progress of the initiatives; these include information on how customers are progressing in meeting their identified needs, and on the cohesion and effectiveness of the partnerships. The required tasks of the WIRED regions in the US, the regional councils in Finland, and regional development strategies in France echo these strategic planning steps.

Performance measures

Information is the glue that helps organisations within a network bond together. Information needs to flow both vertically among the various levels of government and within agencies and horizontally across the partners within a local area. Sharing this information across partnering organisations means that these organisations must speak the same language in terms of purpose and performance outcomes, and must trust their partners in accepting their information to be accurate and their experience relevant.

Performance measures should reflect desired outcomes, and not necessarily required processes. For instance, in the workforce system, one of the desired outcomes is putting people into jobs. Therefore, one of the performance measures should be whether or not a participant in the workforce programme received a job. The interventions that a person received from participating in the programme are important, and good practice requires that the effectiveness of interventions is continuously monitored. However, the final measure of success is whether they helped participants find jobs.

In the US, WIA focuses on three performance measures: entered employment, retention, and earnings levels. All local and state workforce boards are held accountable for achieving minimum thresholds for each measure. The thresholds are negotiated first between the federal government and the states; and then the states, once their thresholds have been established, negotiate with their local workforce boards in order to meet their state thresholds. Performance measures are published quarterly, and failure to meet these thresholds may result in funds being withheld.

The UK's Jobcentre Plus monitors performance of five target areas. The target areas include job outcome, monetary value of fraud and error, employer outcome, customer service level, and claims processing. For the job outcome target, performance is measured in terms of points. Points are allocated for each person Jobcentre Plus helps into work according to the employment or benefit status of the customer. Customers are placed in one of five priority customer groups. Those in Group 1, which has the highest priority, receive 12 points for finding a job; those in Group 5, with the lowest priority, receive one point. Extra points can be earned if the successful customer resides in one of 903 disadvantaged wards. Performance in the other four target areas is measured in a more conventional way. For instance, the employer outcome target is measured as the percentage of employers placing their vacancies with Jobcentre Plus who have a positive outcome. A summary of performance against target is published quarterly for the nation and for each office. Target points are established for each category for each programme year, and the success of the local office and of the staff are judged as to whether or not they met their goal. Funding and even staff compensation and promotion is based on meeting performance targets.

Jobcentre Plus has also established performance indicators for their strategic partners. Recently, the UK government has committed to developing a single, coherent performance framework for local governments working within this partnership. The framework is comprised of 200 performance indicators, from which the partnerships can choose up to 35 targets which they consider to best describe their priorities for their region. Once chosen, the partnerships are held accountable for meeting their agreed upon targets.

Establishing a common basis for defining purpose and objectives is not always easy, since different organisations may focus on different aspects of the challenges facing an individual who is pursuing employment options. The organisations may come from different professional disciplines, such as welfare care workers working with business developers. The cultures of various organisations may also differ in how information is shared. Businesses are unaccustomed to the high level of public transparency required of government agencies, and they resist the oversight and accountability of government. Government agencies are often reluctant to share information about their customers with other agencies. Even if agencies were willing to share information, at some level of aggregation, their data management systems oftentimes reside on computer platforms that are incompatible across departments. In fact, some of the first "whole of government" initiatives focused on rationalising computer systems across agencies. Australia justified their information technology initiative by stating that "information sharing plays a critical role in generating better decision making and programme delivery" (Commonwealth of Australia Management Advisory Committee, 2004). They go on to say that an agency's approach to the management of its information must be driven by its business requirements.

Also, conflicting expectations about performance outcomes from the central government may thwart co-ordination efforts. For instance, while federal and state agencies appear to be pursuing workforce programmes, their respective approaches may differ enough to cause confusion at the local level. The federal government may emphasise quick re-entry into a job regardless of the ability to find a good job match, whereas the state may emphasise training as a means of retooling for high-demand jobs. The state, since it receives funding from the federal government, is obliged to follow their performance expectations, which places a high premium on entered employment. The state, stressing increased skills, places more weight on earnings and retention. Local workforce offices, answering to two masters with conflicting goals, may be confused by the inconsistent performance standards and frustrated by the inability to meet the expectations of both.

Mechanisms/incentives

Networks must also create mechanisms that govern the way in which participants interact. These include sets of incentives, rewards and sanctions that are aligned with the network's objectives and goals. Organisations within networks interact in two basic ways – market exchanges or bargaining. The market exchanges occur typically when government agencies contract for services from other agencies on non-governmental organisations. In this relationship, formal contracts are drawn up stipulating the services that are provided, the number of individuals served, and the cost per service.

Consistent with performance-based objectives, the preferred situation would be for these contracts to also include incentives or sanctions based upon the performance measures.

Furthermore, the mechanisms must be transparent, standardised, and robust enough to maintain interoperability of the entire joined-up network. Eggars and Goldsmith (2004) underscore the interconnectedness of network partners and the need to establish basic business rules that they can all understand and follow: "Networked government typically involves co-ordination between multiple levels of government, non-profit organisations, and for-profit companies. Poor performance by any one organisation within the network, or the breakdown of the relationships between any two organisations within the network, can imperil the performance of the whole." Therefore, partners within the network must have transparent mechanisms for collecting and reporting performance. Since accountability runs vertically and horizontally, the performance and accountability systems must do the same.

An example of bargaining across horizontal partnerships is the US's WIA system. It incorporates performance-based incentives in their formal contracts with subcontractors. The UK's Jobcentre Plus offers an example of a vertical market-exchanged mechanism, in which the central government agency holds local offices and their staff accountable for their performance through their point system.

Bargaining within the network can take place either vertically or horizontally. Vertically, subordinate agencies or local governments may negotiate with central government agencies with respect to performance measures, service delivery, and other policy or administrative responsibilities. As mentioned earlier, the degree to which negotiations take place depends upon the amount of authority and responsibility that is shared among the participants within the network. The US WIA system offers an example of a hybrid approach, incorporating both bargaining and market mechanisms. The US Department of Labor negotiates performance thresholds with state governments and state governments in turn negotiate thresholds with local workforce boards. Once goals are negotiated, a small portion of the funding to the states and to the local WIBs is contingent upon meeting their performance goals.

Horizontally, a network can establish informal relationships through memoranda of understanding, or even less formal relationships. And this can occur not only at the local level but also at the state or central government levels. California's RWPEDA, for example, required memoranda of understanding between the four state agencies in charge of workforce, education, and economic development programmes. The MOUs stipulated that the agencies would develop jointly a strategic plan that co-ordinated the activities of the four departments. The MOUs also set up task forces across the four agencies to ensure that the strategic plan was developed and implemented. At the local level, workforce investment boards under WIA set up MOUs with local service organisations in order to provide a continuum of services to workforce programme participants. Oftentimes, these participants need services that go beyond what are available under the workforce programme, so the MOUs establish ways in which individuals can be referred to other agencies to receive assistance with tacking substance abuse, child care and other social services. Workforce investment boards may also work closely with local economic development organisations, but these relationships may be less formal with the workforce investment boards serving as conveners or facilitators when bringing together other organisations to address specific issues.

Jobcentre Plus, for example, works closely with local partners through Local Area Agreements (LAAs). LAAs set out priorities for a local area agreed upon between the central government and the local area (the local authority and Local Strategic Partnership) and other key partners at the local level. LAAs form the key vehicle for the delivery of national and local outcomes at the local level and form the basis for the single local authority performance management framework. All central government funding for local authorities will be in support of the outcomes defined through targets and indicators in LAAs, giving local authorities considerable flexibility in how they use their resources (UK Department for Communities and Local Government, 2006). In 2008, the UK government made significant changes to the LAAs which promise to enable local partners to respond more flexibly to local needs and to reduce the amount of top-down control from central government.

Finally, the mechanisms must allow partnering organisations to manage and share risk. Outsourcing to private organisations transfers some of the risk normally assumed by government to the private sector in terms of meeting their contractual obligations, specifically performance-based contracts. The question is not how much risk to transfer to the private sector. Rather, it is what is the optimal type and amount of risk. Governments typically stand ready to assume risk for responding to natural disasters, for example. However, governments at times are less willing to assume the risk of trying new practices or approaches, particularly those agencies or organisations that are subordinate to central government agencies. Sharing risk through a diversified approach across a network can prove helpful. A diversified approach is one in which the various agencies experiment with different innovative practices, as opposed to everyone pursuing the same practice. The chances that all the new practices will fail are much lower than the likelihood that a single new approach adopted by everyone may not meet expectations. The US system in which states and local areas have some discretion to design innovative workforce programmes has been seen as a way to encourage innovation through a more diversified approach that reduces risk.

When complexities are high and responsibility unclear, there is a proliferation of structures to try to create controls over management. The creation of boards, taskforces, commissions, interdepartmental committees is a typical response to managing complexities. However, these add extra layers of complexity and fragmentation to an already fragmented system in which responsibilities are somewhat uncertain.

Staff development at all levels

Another requirement for successful horizontal co-ordination is the development of talented staff at all levels of government. For staff to carry out their responsibilities within a network in which authority is shared at various levels of government, staff must possess the talent and knowledge to function independently within the network. To be effective partners, organisations must also have competent staff that understand how the organisation fits within the goals and objectives of the partnership and can carry out their responsibilities within that partnership. Staff must therefore be trained not only in providing the services their particular organisation specialises in, but also in understanding how to be meaningful participants in a partnership arrangement.

The Canada School of Public Service recommends that staff be trained and selected according to their "horizontal co-ordination" skills. These skills include financial management, mediation and negotiation skills, creativity, and patience. Eggars and Goldsmith (2004) add risk analysis, contract management, interpersonal communications, and team building to the list. The School of Public Service also recommends creating a special unit within departments tasked with supporting horizontal co-ordination through training advice, good practices, and promotion of a horizontal culture. It is important to recognise that even though the appropriate structure and mechanisms are in place to achieve horizontal co-ordination, the likelihood of success is low unless staff are trained to take ownership in the objectives and goals agreed upon within the network and are instilled with a culture of co-ordination. Eggers and Goldsmith (2004) conclude that building human resource capacity requires a "full-blown cultural transformation", which is "nothing less than changing the definition of what it means to be a public employee."

Issues related to workforce development and economic development co-ordination

The lessons learned from broad government reforms to improve horizontal co-ordination are pertinent to the efforts to improve co-ordination between workforce development and economic development programmes. The same issues regarding responding to the needs of workers and businesses at the local level and in balancing flexibility and accountability are shared by these efforts and others. Now that the framework for examining the question of decentralisation and horizontal co-ordination has been established and lessons have been gleaned from other reform attempts, the two specific issues regarding workforce and economic development can be addressed. These issues are: i) the difficulty of achieving co-ordination because of the vertical structure of public institutions and the pressure on these institutions to contribute to national policy goals; and ii) the practice of giving preference to actions that are part of broad long-term local strategies at the expense of those yielding more immediate results for individual policy areas, to make a real difference at the local level.

Vertical government structure and national policy goals

The first issue can be addressed with respect to three of the elements of successful co-ordination: i) the structure of the network; ii) determination of which level of government is best suited to perform required functions; and iii) distribution of authority within the network. For workforce development and economic development programmes, the importance of responding to the needs of workers and businesses at the local level has been well established. Therefore, a bottom-up approach, with shared authority among the agencies in the network, is an appropriate structure for gathering information about local needs and acting upon it. The degree of tension between having the flexibility to serve local needs and complying with national policy and administrative guidelines depends upon the extent to which the central government is involved in these activities. For workforce programmes, central governments in most countries take a dominant role. For economic development activities, more often than not, local entities lead these efforts. Therefore, in countries that follow these practices, the tension is primarily within the workforce development system.

This leads to the next key element – the level of government that is best suited to perform various functions. We have already established that local governments (local offices) are better able to monitor the needs of workers. On the other hand, it is recognised that the central government is better equipped to deal with equity issues and has greater capacity to raise funds through taxation than local governments. Therefore, the question is how to reconcile equity issues of administering employment services fairly to individuals throughout a nation while recognising that workers in some areas require more and different types of services than those in other locales. The answer lies in setting up the proper goals and objectives, which are based on the desired outcomes of the workers and not on a notion of required processes.

The central government can determine the proper national goals, such as placing as many people as possible into jobs that match their skills. In this way, accountability is first focused on the customer and secondarily on the budget statements of each entity.

The performance levels and standards can be negotiated with the state and local entities based upon local circumstances. The central government should then allow the state and local entities to determine the best combination of services and the best way to administer services, while encouraging local areas to experiment with innovative approaches. The central government should also provide incentives and funding that encourages local governments or agencies in charge of providing employment services to partner with other government agencies to co-ordinate the range of services provided to individuals beyond those that are directly under the authority of central government's workforce agencies. In addition, the central government should provide technical assistance to help states and local entities develop strategies and administer services. They should also take a leadership role in training staff, both in the central agencies and in local governments, to acquire the skills needed to create a culture of horizontal co-ordination.

If for some countries workforce development agencies are also strongly linked to a central government agency, similar arrangements should be considered in order to balance flexibility and accountability within that system as well. The key areas are the proper distribution of authority within the network and a focus on performance measures that centre on the outcomes of customers and not on required procedures.

Once that proper balance is struck, local entities are less encumbered to form horizontal partnerships. Establishing meaningful horizontal partnerships at the local level requires all the elements discussed in the previous section, with leadership and strategic planning topping the list. For those programmatic areas that have strong central government agencies, such as workforce programmes, it is critical that horizontal co-ordination is achieved at the central government level so that goals and objectives are aligned vertically and horizontally throughout the network of organisations. The structure set up by California's RWPEDA using memoranda of understanding and high-level task forces illustrates this approach.

Trade-off between long-term local strategies and short-term objectives

The second issue is the trade-off between broad long-term local strategies and narrower, short-term objectives that yield more immediate results. One of the lessons distilled from the broad government reforms seeking greater horizontal co-ordination is the realisation that it is difficult to muster support for cross-cutting initiatives if the goals are too abstract and grandiose. Rather, they must be specific, manageable, and measurable. If not, staff may lose sight of their objectives and lack the ownership needed to make co-ordination work, and political representatives may lose interest in the programme and reduce funding or restructure (or even end) the programme. For co-ordinating workforce development and economic development functions, it is a long-term endeavour that must be sustained over time. In this case, the balance is between recognising and appreciating longer-term goals while establishing short-term performance milestones that are properly aligned with the longer-term vision for the co-ordinated effort.

Using the US WIA programme as an example, the central government established six long-term goals: universal access, integrated and co-ordinated services, customer focus and empowerment, increased accountability and efficiency through performance monitoring, strengthened local decision making through WIBs, and enhanced state and local flexibility. Simultaneously, they created customer-focused performance measures that were aligned with these goals and that were monitored quarterly. They also eventually created an information system (referred to as the WIA standard record database, WIASRD) so that the reporting information is standardised across all states and the more than 600 workforce investment areas.

Conclusion

Successful co-ordination of workforce development and economic development programmes can help local areas better compete in a global economy by responding more effectively to the needs of workers and businesses, encouraging more innovative practices and entrepreneurship, promoting social cohesion, leveraging government resources by partnering with non-government organisations, and instilling more local ownership in local decision-making and strategic initiatives. However, the potential of horizontal co-ordination among local agencies and organisations has not yet been fully realised. Based upon lessons learned from efforts by several countries to achieve greater horizontal co-ordination among government agencies at all levels of government, this Chapter concludes that it will not be achieved through a simple restructuring of government, but rather it requires a cultural transformation among management, staff, and policy makers. This requires attention to customers, the balance between accountability and flexibility, appropriate mechanisms and incentives, performance-based monitoring, strategic planning and goal setting, alignment, strong leadership, and trust among partners.

Not only government but also the private sector has recognised the benefits of horizontal co-ordination. The emergence of global supply chains is built on the principles of horizontal co-ordination in which a dominant firm provides strategic guidance. Horizontal co-ordination takes place between affiliates of multinational corporations, between different business functions and within individual units. It allows firms to be more responsive to external changes, to focus on the core business while offering them the scope and scale of the collective network.

Key elements gleaned from these government reform efforts have been successfully practiced by the private sector as well. A set of principles that has been widely used to identify best practice among organisations was developed by a group of business experts for the US Department of Commerce, as a tool to aid businesses, government organisations, and non-profit organisations in improving their performance. Each year since its inception in 1988, the Department of Commerce has conferred the coveted Malcolm Baldrige National Quality Award on a handful of businesses and organisations, each of which has gone through a gruelling process of self-evaluation and external evaluation of their management and workforce practices. The criteria include leadership, strategic planning, customer focus, information and analysis, human resource development, process management, and business results. It is easy to see the similarities between these criteria and those described for successful networks and horizontal co-ordination.

Achieving effective partnerships, both horizontally and vertically, within a network of public and private providers, is a long, transformational journey. It involves increasing the ability to commingle individual funding sources, reducing programme restrictions, overcoming turf issues, collapsing hierarchies in order to empower those making decisions and providing the services, and providing continual feedback on the effectiveness of efforts. The reward for successful partnerships and the integration of the functions of workforce development and economic development is developing a workforce that is better prepared to meet the needs of local businesses, and thus to meet the challenges of an increasingly competitive global economy that all local economies face.

Bibliography

Bakvis, H. and L. Juillet (2004), *The Horizontal Challenge: Line Department, Central Agencies, and Leadership*, Canada School of Public Service.

Barnow, B.S. and C.T. King (2005), *The Workforce Investment Act in Eight States*, US Department of Labor, Employment and Training Administration Occasional Paper 2005-01 (February), Washington DC.

Boissard, S. (2008), "La dimension territoriale des politiques de l'emploi – Le cas de la France" (The Territorial dimension of Employment Policies – The French Case), presentation at the OECD Conference on Decentralisation and Co-ordination: *The Twin Challenges of Labour Market Policy*, Venice, 17-19 April 2008.

Chandler, J.A., "Joined Up Government or Determining Priorities", unpublished and undated manuscript, Sheffield Hallam University.

Canada Deputy Minister Task Force on Horizontal Issues (1996), "Managing Horizontal Policy Issues".

Chao, E. (2008), "Remarks Prepared for Delivery by US Secretary of Labor Elaine L. Chao, OECD Summit on Decentralization of Labour Market Policy", 18 April 2008, States News Service, *www.highbeam.com*, last accessed April 2008.

Cronberg, Tarja (2008), presentation at the OECD Conference on Decentralisation and Co-ordination: The Twin Challenges of Labour Market Policy, Venice, 17-19 April 2008.

Commonwealth of Australia Management Advisory Committee (2004), Connecting Government: Whole of Government Responses to Australia's Priority Challenges, Commonwealth of Australia, Canberra.

Dafflon, B. (1999), "Fiscal Federalism in Switzerland: A Survey of Constitutional Issues, Budget Responsibility and Equalization", *SDC/World Bank Partnership on Decentralisation and Governance*, Berne, 8-9 December.

Eggers, W.D. and S. Goldsmith (2004), "Government by Network: The New Public Management Imperative", Deloitte Research and the Ash Institute for Democratic Governance at the John F. Kennedy School of Government at Harvard University, USA.

Giguère, S. (2008), "A Broader Agenda for Workforce Development", in S. Giguère (ed.), *More than Just Jobs: Workforce Development in a Skills-based Economy*, OECD Publishing, Paris.

Greffe, X. (2008), "France: Bridging Regional Training and Local Employment,"in S. Giguere (ed.) *More than Just Jobs: Workforce Development in a Skills-based Economy*, OECD Publishing, Paris.

International Labour Organisation (1998), "Global Production and Local Jobs: New Perspectives on Enterprise Networks, Employment, and Local Development Policy", discussion paper for international workshop, Geneva 9-10 March.

Johnson, B. (2005), "Strategies for Successful Joined Up Government Initiatives", John Curtin Institute for Public Policy, Institute of Public Administration of Australia Department of Premier and Cabinet.

Ling, T. (2002), "Delivering Joined-up Government in the UK: Dimensions, Issue and Problems", *Public Administration*, 80(4), pp. 615-642.

OECD (1999), *Decentralising Employment Policy: New Trends and Challenges*, OECD Publishing, Paris.

Osborne, D. and T. Gaebler (1992), *Reinventing Government*, Addison-Wesley, Reading, Massachusetts.

Peters, B.G. (1998), "Managing Horizontal Government: The Politics of Co-ordination", Canadian Centre for Management Development.

Puljiz, J. (2003), "The Role of Economic Development Agencies in Promoting the Development of Lagging Areas of Croatia – the Case of LEDAs", in *Economic Development on the Local and Regional Level*, Friedrich Ebert Stiftung, Zagreb.

Stoker, G. (2003), "Joined Up Public Services: A Briefing Note for IPEG's Public Service Cluster", unpublished manuscript, University of Manchester.

UK Cabinet Office Performance and Innovation Unit (2000), *Reaching Out: The Role of Central Government at Regional and Local Level*, Central Office of Information, London.

UK Department for Communities and Local Government (2006), "Strong and Prosperous Communities, The Local Government White Paper", The Stationery Office, UK.

Van Empel, C. (2000), "Local Economic Development Agencies, Instrument for Reconciliation and Reintegration in Post-conflict Croatia", ILO, Geneva.

ISBN 978-92-64-05918-4
Flexible Policy for More and Better Jobs
© OECD 2009

Chapter 6

What Can Governments Do to Meet Skills and Employability Challenges at the Local Level?

by

Dave Simmonds

The skills and employability of the local labour force are crucial to the ability of economies to respond to labour market shocks and adapt to global change. The quicker that the unemployed can be re-trained for new jobs, the more adaptable a local economy will be. However, a constraint on improving adaptability is the ability of the state to adequately and quickly reform the delivery of training, welfare systems and employability programmes to meet new challenges. A greater emphasis needs to be placed on the personalisation and localisation of service design, planning, and delivery. Personalisation is needed to combine different forms of support required by people with multiple barriers, and localisation is needed to empower local partners to design interventions and direct resources to meet local employer needs and target the most deprived areas and people. Decentralisation appears to be a necessary condition for joining up services at the point of delivery and for disadvantaged areas to devise solutions to tackle their specific problems.

Introduction

The increased interest by governments in the extent to which skills and employability policy should be devolved has raised important questions about how local services are managed. If the primary motivation for devolution is to improve the effectiveness of interventions then the framework for devolution must create the conditions for local partners to deliver this improvement.

However, this might not always be the case. The uneasy tension between the requirements of different levels of governance can mean that the capacity and powers of the local level are often compromised. If the potential of decentralisation is to be realised then governments have to consider the most effective ways that local areas can identify and meet skills and employability challenges.

OECD countries either already have devolved frameworks for the management of public employment services or have been experimenting with the degree of responsibility different levels of governance are given, and this is often being driven by wider public sector reform principles. This chapter draws heavily on UK experience and considers the arguments for devolution of employment and skills policy in their own right.

The importance of workforce adaptability

One of the primary drivers for countries to improve their training and employability infra-structure is the need to increase the adaptability of their economies to global economic, environmental, and political change. Increasingly successful economies will be those that can quickly adapt to external trends and shocks. Whilst some nations have had the ability to absorb external shocks (such as the recent global slowdown) because of their natural resources, accumulated wealth or strength in specific markets, there are now few that do not experience the increasing impact of global change. Even those countries with strong global markets realise that they have to do more to remain competitive and increase productivity.

The adaptability of the workforce will therefore be a critical element in this drive and is one reason why governments are introducing more flexible labour market regulations – removing perceived barriers to change by workforces and the labour market as a whole. However, adaptability needs to be considered at a number of different levels. National governments set the legal framework for employers and trade unions but adaptability has to happen at the level of the individual company. Employers have to be empowered and incentivised to innovate and introduce change. In the future, the extent of adaptability of employers in a local economy is likely to a measure of success – the more adaptable a local economy the more likely it will be successful.

How do governments encourage local economies to be more adaptable? There are a number of ways in which this can be done, but the skill levels and employability of the workforce has to be a key driver. The simple definition of how long "structural unemployment" persists is the amount of time required to re-train the unemployed for new jobs – the quicker this can be done the more adaptable a local economy will be. However, it is not just about responding to job losses – companies and workforces also have to adjust to new production processes and new ideas in the knowledge economy. Innovative and successful companies are those that manage these adjustments quickly and effectively.

National governments therefore need to establish legislative and institutional frameworks that permit local economies to adjust quickly. Achieving this is not easy given the complex inter-relationship of different policy objectives embedded in skills and employability systems. Governments are mainly in control of the institutional and delivery infra-structure and this can be a barrier if public services do not adjust with sufficient speed. Indeed it can be argued that national governments can slow down the rate of adjustment of local economies because of the need to achieve other policy priorities. Institutional reform to achieve different policy objectives often leads to a complex multi-layering of organisations, partnerships and initiatives because different parts of the system adjust at different speeds. The consequences of this complexity is felt at the local level where there is often a confusion of policy and delivery responsibility and a lack of focus for the design and purpose of local services.

Why local control has become more important

These issues are more important in many countries today because of the changed characteristics of those who are out of work and the increased demands of adaptability on those who are in work. Before the recent economic crisis, lower levels of jobseekers had led to a higher proportion of the workless having more barriers to employment and/or receiving inactive benefits. Figure 6.1 shows this shift in the UK with unemployment benefits declining and a persistent increase in Incapacity Benefit (for those with disabilities and health problems).

In the United Kingdom this led to a reform of Incapacity Benefits in October 2008, and even before this there were already signs that claimant

Figure 6.1. **Changes in key benefits since 1979 (United Kingdom)**

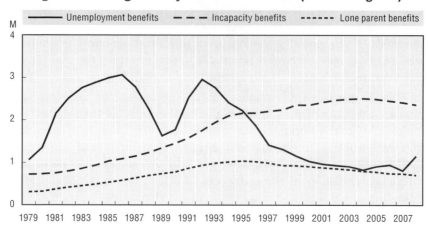

Source: Department for Work and Pensions, Department for Social Security, Quarterly Statistical Enquiries (2008).

numbers were reducing. A recent report by the OECD (2007) on four countries highlighted the shift many countries are undergoing to provide more for people with disabilities and health problems. It concluded that in all four countries (Spain, Luxembourg, United Kingdom and Australia) more people claim disability benefits when unemployment is high and continue their claims when the labour market eases. To stop this cycle, the OECD recommends that governments should reform both disability and unemployment benefit schemes at the same time.

However, this is difficult to do especially where the numbers on disability benefits have continued to grow and there is a large stock of people that have been on disability benefits for a long time. In the United Kingdom there were in 2008 four times as many people on disabled benefits than on unemployment benefit. The problem that arises is reconciling the conditions for receipt of different benefit payments and providing opportunities for all claimants and at the same time preventing perverse incentives to claim a particular benefit. There is therefore likely to be an equalisation, over a period of time, of the level of payments and the conditions for receiving welfare payments.

The challenge of reducing economic inactivity is significant and it can take longer to implement change in welfare systems and public services than anticipated, or indeed needed by individuals. The legal and institutional infra-structure required to manage high levels of unemployment (as opposed to inactivity) was difficult to change and most countries have had to take an incremental approach for a variety of political and delivery reasons. For example, in the United Kingdom despite the introduction of new support for people joining Incapacity Benefit, the majority of provision and expenditure has still been focused on the mandatory jobseeker New Deals, which has meant large parts of the infrastructure (mainstream delivery, contract management and policy) took time to gear up to the challenge.

A basic assumption behind much current skills and employability reform is that new capacity needs to be built, one that is more in tune with:

● Delivering outcomes for economically inactive people.

● Meeting the needs of local economies and employers.

● Fitting with public sector reform principles.

● Working within resource constraints.

In a recent report to the United Kingdom government, Freud (2007) highlighted the sort of change needed:

> [A]s the [United Kingdom] Government moves beyond its traditional groups and further into the very hardest to help, the current regime will have to evolve further. It will need to move from a traditional approach based on client groups and specific symptoms to one based on individual needs.

Experience of the shift from "traditional groups" to the economically inactive has thrown up some key lessons:

● There is a wide diversity of the economically inactive population in terms of personal characteristics, household types, specific barriers, neighbourhood and motivation.

● There are fewer mandatory requirements for inactive claimants and this means a greater emphasis on voluntary activity.

● The extent of labour market detachment is significantly more than that experienced by the majority of unemployed claimants – the duration of claims on inactive benefits is very significantly longer than unemployed claimants.

● The high degree of geographical concentration both nationally and locally.

● Solutions to some significant barriers remain outside the direct control of employment and skills services, *e.g.* health and childcare services.

● The limited extent to which government measures can reach some the inactive.

● The high incidences of child poverty within inactive households.

Collectively, these mean significant challenges to policymakers and service providers at all levels of governance. Central to reform is the recognition that services need to become more *personalised* – providing what individuals need to increase their employability, rather than what programmes will or won't provide.

Box 6.1. **Lessons and challenges: the Catalan experience**

The past decade saw a significant rise in the Catalan employment – in 1998, it was just 58% and, in 2008, it was 72%. More than 1 million new jobs were created in Catalonia, many of which went to women, with their employment rate rising from 44% to 63%. The unemployment rate more than halved in the decade – falling from 16% to 7%.

This improvement has occurred in a period when Spain has been both devolving employment and skills and introducing more flexibility in the labour market. Since the mid-1990s Spain has devolved most responsibilities for the planning and delivery of active labour market measures, but within a national framework. Each Spanish region is responsible for:

● Planning of active labour market policies.

● Supply and demand matching.

● Fostering and execution of active labour market policies.

● Promotion of local development initiatives.

Local authorities within regions have devolved responsibility for some employment programmes and economic development initiatives and Catalonia is encouraging more decentralisation below the regional level.

Spain and Catalonia are striving to increase the level of vocational training and qualifications which are presently significantly below that of the European Union average. There is a low participation rate in vocational and on-going training, and more connection and progression is needed between initial, occupational and on-going vocational training. To achieve this Catalonia is encouraging more legal and policy flexibility but also stressing the need for co-ordination and identification of strategic priorities for the region.

A new Vocational Training Plan (2008-10) is aiming to deliver more and better initial vocational training with a 40% increase in vocational training participants. The training for unemployed people will focus on replacement and new skills acquisition for industries experiencing labour shortages and emerging sectors. To deliver this Catalonia is promoting partnerships, particularly between local administrations, employers and regional government.

There is a new emphasis on a partnership between cities and the region to:

● Decentralise active labour market policies to the neighbourhood.

● Join up issues related to equal opportunities and social cohesion with economic and local development.

● Give more flexibility in programmes.

Box 6.1. **Lessons and challenges: the Catalan experience** *(cont.)*

To facilitate effective decentralisation Catalonia stresses the need for good information and evaluation for decision-making. A new Labour Observatory is being established to gather and analyse local information about labour market issues. This helps assure the participation of social and economic stakeholders and aids good decision-making.

Catalonia is planning a new kind of decentralisation of labour market policies as a way to increase flexibility and efficiency. Employment Pacts are also being encouraged between local administrations, trade unions, employers and other stakeholders. There will also be more participation by stakeholders in the Catalonia Employment Service.

The lessons from Catalonia are:

- There is more efficiency and social impact when policies are addressed to specific areas.
- Training is a way to increase employability and competitiveness.
- Programmes must adjust skills and professional careers to labour market changes.
- Equality is a key factor for competitiveness and social cohesion.
- New challenges require more consensus to define labour market policies.

However, Catalonia recognises that decentralisation challenges remain. There will need to be more focus on local administrations, neighbourhoods and target groups with the highest unemployment risk at the local level. Finally, more and better partnerships are needed with local administrations and social and economic stakeholders.

Source: Serna Calvo (2008).

The need to personalise has been recognised for some time. This has been characterised by introducing a stronger emphasis on advice and support by public employment service staff and programmes that are geared to individual needs rather than stipulated programme actions. In the Netherlands, Personal Accounts have been introduced that allows a claimant and a Personal Advisor to purchase the support needed to increase employability. In Denmark a new programme called "A New Chance for Everyone" was started in 2006 (see Box 4.2) – everyone who has received different forms of passive benefits for more than a year will have their situation reviewed to assess how they can best be helped into employment or education. The increased use in a number of countries of so called "black box" provision (where contractors are paid on outcomes rather than processes) is also intended to provide more personalised solutions.

When personalising support there will need to be an increased awareness of the nature, extent, and quality of services that should be available at the local level for workless people. This also means there needs to an increased national, local, and contractor understanding of "what works" in terms of provision and delivery.

Personalising service reform is not easy given the multiple objectives across different government departments. Services and initiatives for skills and the workless tend to be separately planned and delivered to: manage and reduce the claimant count; to regenerate deprived communities; and to increase the skills and productivity of the workforce. This may make sense at the national, or even regional, level but makes less sense at the local frontline where policymakers and service providers attempt to solve local economic and social problems, personalise services and meet targets. The different objectives give rise to distinct approaches – work first, human capital (skills), and area-based regeneration initiatives. Each has led to controversy and debate, but there now needs to be an emphasis on what can be learned from each approach and how they can be brought together to improve delivery.

But what works in terms of specific interventions to improve employment and skills? Recent United Kingdom research (Hasluck and Green, 2007) has highlighted the nature of interventions that work:

- Interventions which are holistic rather than focusing only on one aspect of employability.
- Providing the right support at the right time for individuals.
- Active outreach to engage workless people who otherwise might not take up opportunities.
- The quality, enthusiasm and commitment of support staff.
- Personal advisors with flexibility to deliver specific needs.
- Engendering and maintaining motivation, especially through voluntary involvement rather than mandatory programmes.
- Job search activity is central – if people don't look for work they won't find work.
- Active engagement with employers – being "demand led".
- Providing continuity of support between job search, work experience and training.
- Tackling basic skills problems at an early stage.
- Allowing continuity of training, in and out of employment.

However, it has to be stressed that "what works" varies between different groups of people, for localities and by what employers are demanding. Understanding what interventions work helps to minimise the risk of worklessness but it does not mean that it will work for everyone all of the time. To get a further performance gain it is argued that there should be the notion of "what works" for each individual. This again leads to a stress on personalisation rather than designing specific initiatives or programmes.

Delivering greater personalisation requires re-thinking how a number of different services are delivered and targeted, as well as how people can be better informed of available opportunities. This, at a minimum, means:

- More accessible and better information about opportunities.
- A universal citizen's advice service on careers, skills and employment.
- Better co-ordination of existing mainstream and specialist services, spanning the needs of disadvantaged groups.
- Streamlined access to support which minimises bureaucracy and waiting times.
- Improved links with employers to understand their recruitment and training requirements and encourage them to change practices that may restrict access to jobs and training by disadvantaged groups.
- "One-stop shops" or "unified gateways" which act as access points for communities and for employers.
- The number and quality of "intermediaries" or "gatekeepers"i.e. personal advisors and skills brokers.

Most of this is best planned at the local level – allowing local areas to determine the right mix of services and the best use of available resources. This implies that local policy makers have to be constantly reviewing the characteristics and geography of workless people, the nature of employer demand, and any skills deficit in the workforce – and developing strategies and services to match the supply and demand for skilled labour. See for example the case of Catalonia in Box 6.1.

Figure 6.2 characterises the skills management challenge in the United Kingdom. Whilst this figure has been used to describe the national challenge, it can be applied at any level of governance. If it is true that the "frontline" of management should be at the local level (understanding needs, deploying resources, and measuring performance and impact) then "local management" need the capacity and powers to understand the inputs and deliver the outputs to secure a gain in performance.

Whilst it may be readily accepted that to deliver greater personalisation the level at which strategies are developed, and services planned, is vitally important, it is the degree of variation of local economic circumstances that provides a critical economic justification. Whilst the main target groups are common across a nation their degree of geographical concentration can vary significantly. These variations are often a reflection of the different speeds and

Figure 6.2. **Skills management in the United Kingdom**

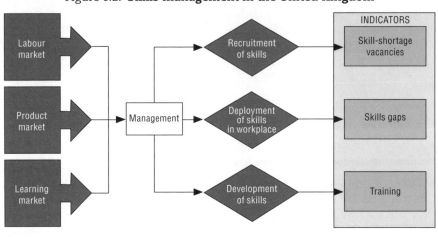

Source: Leitch, S. (2006).

extent to which local economies have been able to adapt to macro-economic change, as well as changes in the composition of the local labour force.

Figure 6.3 shows the divergence of skill levels across regions and nations in the United Kingdom, and within each English region and Scotland, Wales and Northern Ireland, there are also further equally wide disparities. This

Figure 6.3. **Highest qualification held in UK regions**

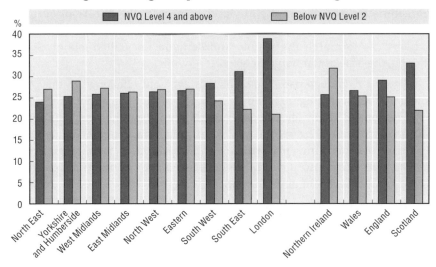

Note: Base = UK working age population; Below Level 2 excludes non-classed qualifications (including overseas).
Source: Labour Force Survey (Oct.-Dec. 2008), Office for National Statistics (2004).

divergence also helps to explain the productivity gaps that exist between parts of the United Kingdom and with other economies. Porter and Ketels (2003) analysis on the causes of the United Kingdom's lagging national competitiveness cited regional and local differences among the reasons for poor productivity:

- Large regional differences in the quality of the business environment and economic performance.
- Limited presence or effectiveness of institutions encouraging regional and local collaboration.

London is the main example of a region with wide variations that inhibit growth of productivity and meeting social justice objectives. London has large numbers of people with high qualifications but also high concentrations of people with low qualifications and multiple labour market disadvantages. These concentrations help explain why London has one of the lowest employment rates in the United Kingdom but the highest proportion of people with high qualifications. This is one reason why, in 2007, the United Kingdom government has devolved some statutory powers for skills to the Mayor of London – the first English region to get more powers.

In addition to divergences in skill levels there are significant variations in the nature of employer demand, and responsiveness to employers mainly requires a localised approach. Finally, the capacity and quality of the supply-side infra-structure for employment and skills will also vary, which will be part of the explanation for variations in performance. In the larger cities performance can be lower than the national average and therefore not providing the capacity to close the skills and employment gap. In the United Kingdom, all of the major cities (with one exception) have job outcomes from national programmes which are below the national average. This is something which cities themselves are eager to correct, and is part of the objectives of the new United Kingdom initiative called City Strategies.

Viewed from the demand-side the need for devolution is further reinforced. Figure 6.4 shows the jobs growth needed in United Kingdom cities for the country to reach an 80% employment rate (the government's employment rate aspiration). The job growth needed in London is so large that it is split into inner and outer London. However, all major cities in the United Kingdom require significant numbers of new jobs, and whilst the state of the national economy has an obvious influence on the ability of local economies to create jobs, each of the cities have developed their own plans and strategies for how to attract employers and stimulate their economies.

The extent of variation of local employment rates for the United Kingdom is shown in Figure 6.5. It plots the employment rate for every local authority from the lowest to the highest, which range from 53% to 90% – a gap of

Figure 6.4. **UK cities: Increase in employment needed to reach 80% of residents in work**

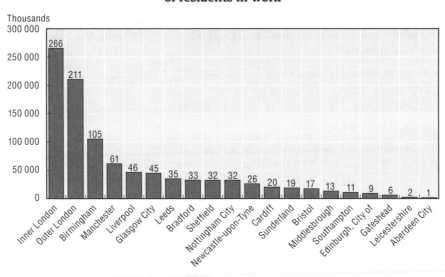

Source: Inclusion analysis of Annual Population Survey (July 2007-June 2008), UK Office for National Statistics.

Figure 6.5. **Local authority employment rates in Great Britain, 2007-08**

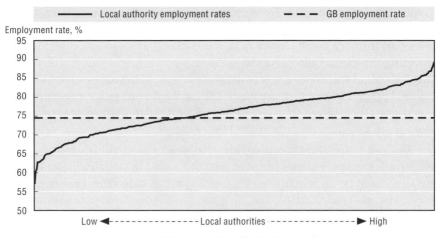

Source: Annual Population Survey (July 2007-June 2008), Office for National Statistics.

37 percentage points. There are just twenty Local Authorities in the drop-off between 65% and 55% at the low end, out of total of over four hundred English Local Authorities.

This gap between the highest and lowest employment areas and the distinctive drop-off at the low end is one reason why the government has a national target to close the gap between the lowest and the highest. In the past the United Kingdom government has done this through high levels of regeneration spending in the lowest employment areas combined with additional employment and skills initiatives, but these have been planned and delivered separately. From 2008, the government has brought together these funds in a new combined "Working Neighbourhood Fund", which will encourage more local strategic planning for how funds are spent.

Strategic choices in commissioning and delivery

Governments have choices about how strategic planning is translated into service delivery. A number of countries (in particular Australia and the Netherlands) take the approach that what happens in the "black box" of service provision should not be the business of government (local or national). Instead, provision should be contracted for on the basis of outcomes and rewards, and contractors (usually in the private and not-for-profit sector) will use "what works" to maximise their rewards. This approach places the onus on government to manage the market effectively so that the desired national and local outcomes are achieved – with a minimum of distortion. Other countries provide the majority of services through the public sector, using their understanding of what works to design interventions which may or may not give flexibility to local offices to meet local needs.

However, these approaches are not necessarily mutually exclusive. In the Netherlands more freedom has recently been given to municipalities to design, contract for, and operate provision for those on social security benefits. This has led to some municipalities bringing back provision under their direct control and ceasing to use contractors to the same extent.

Different models established by governments have led to local partners establishing new combinations of strategic planning, direct service provision, and actions such as providing information brokerage and service co-ordination, and the OECD distinguishes between "devolved" and "integrated" models. In the devolved model powers are given to design and implement policies at the regional or local level. In the integrated model policies and delivery take place within a national framework, usually based on the public employment service and the funding agency for skills training.

In the search for performance gains there are a considerable number of variations across countries in how local areas can exert influence or control. These variations arise as a result of countries modifying their frameworks based on their experience of "what works", as well as their political and cultural attitude to local and centralised control. There does, however, appear to be an increased appreciation that the local dimension is now more important for many economies to tackle deep-seated social and economic problems. At the same time a market-based approach is often layered on top of both models by using a competitive contractor market which is controlled and regulated by different levels of government.

Choices between "devolved" and "integrated", "market-based" and "public service" determine the nature and shape of the institutional framework for planning and delivery. However, in most countries these institutions are persistently in flux as national choices are made – leading to a complex mix of institutions and policy drivers.

Complexity of systems

The inter-related nature of skills and employability systems brings with it a web of institutions that need to work together and communicate at one level or another. Using the United Kingdom as an example demonstrates this complexity. Figure 6.6 shows the number of different government departments, agencies, and stakeholders who all have a direct interest in policy, planning, influencing, and delivering skills and employability services. This is a simplified figure because if the funding and accountability lines are added it becomes even more confusing. The United Kingdom government accepted the recommendations from the Leitch review (2006) that the system should be reformed to make it clearer and more responsive to learners and employers. A new employer led Commission for Employment and Skills has been established to make recommendations about how the institutional framework should be reformed. In addition, individual Skills Accounts are to be introduced that will make the whole system more demand led, as well as drive a better integration of skills and employment services.

The impact of this complexity at the local level means that there are often large numbers of different national funding streams operating in deprived areas, many with similar or complementary objectives. Whilst each national fund may be justified by national policy objectives the danger is that they operate in isolation at the local level and hence diminish impact or lead to confused public services. Local areas also have to absorb the high transaction costs of managing the bureaucracy attached to each fund. The increased use of targets in the United Kingdom has also led to local areas having to reconcile what have often been felt to be (at best) targets that should be aligned or (at worst) targets that are conflicting. Box 6.2 describes similarly how local actors in Belgium are dealing with complexity within their own system produced by differences in regional programming.

FLEXIBLE POLICY FOR MORE AND BETTER JOBS – ISBN 978-92-64-05918-4 – © OECD 2009

Figure 6.6. **UK skills and employment system, 2006**

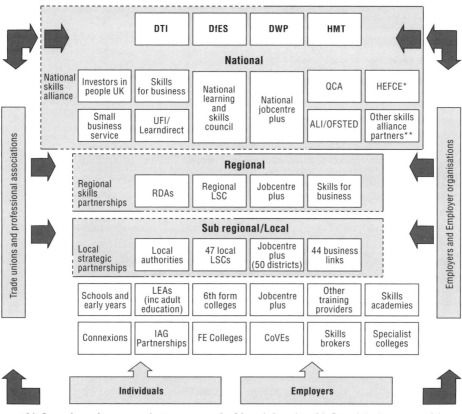

Note: This figure shows the structure in 2006. As a result of the Leitch Review, this figure is in the process of change.
Source: "Skills in the UK: the long-term challenges", *the Leitch Review*, UK HM Treasury, 2005.

Box 6.2. **Belgium: Regional co-operation to overcome complexity**

Belgium is having to tackle the complexity associated with a relatively devolved system. The country is governed by strong autonomous regions which have extensive powers over education, skills and employment. However, it was recognised by the regions that co-operation was needed to overcome the rigidities that this autonomy created in the labour market, for example, each region is responsible for collecting its employer vacancies and does not have to share them with other regions.

In February 2005, the Brussels-Capital region, the Flemish region, the Walloon region, the Flemish and German communities, and the Commission for the French community reached an agreement to co-operate on inter-regional mobility for those seeking work.

Box 6.2. **Belgium: Regional co-operation to overcome complexity** (*cont.*)

The guiding principles of this agreement are:

- The exchange of vacancies.

- Measures to strengthen job-seekers' mobility.

- The promotion of language learning and training.

- Linking of training opportunities.

- Co-operation in instances of mass redundancies.

- An action plan for co-ordination between Brussels and its surrounding areas.

Since the agreement the regions have been developing projects to promote greater flexibility and mobility across Belgium. There is now: an automatic exchange of vacancies; the promotion of language training across regions; a joint plan in the event of mass redundancies; and an inter-regional action plan. In addition, there are a number of bi-lateral accords between regions covering issues of mutual concern. For example, Brussels is co-operating with the surrounding region on a range of projects including the promotion of language training and the harmonisation of training.

Belgium's experience since the 2005 agreement shows that: *i*) research is needed to understand and demonstrate the benefits of horizontal synergies; *ii*) more joint work on local initiatives has quickly developed; *iii*) there is more recognition that formal harmonisation and co-ordination is required between the regions; *iv*) the regions need to develop transparency in communications and the exchange of expertise; and *v*) inter-regional agreements to co-operate are seen as the way forward – if they are linked to operational delivery plans.

Source: Cerexhe (2008).

Why skills and employability need local planning

In summary, the main drivers for reform in the United Kingdom, and many other countries, are:

- Improve adaptability and productivity.

- Achieve social and economic inclusion goals.

- Personalise services.

- Reduce geographic disparities.

- Integration between skills and employment services.

Figure 6.7 shows the dynamics of different influences on further education and skills training in the United Kingdom. Half of the influences are

FLEXIBLE POLICY FOR MORE AND BETTER JOBS – ISBN 978-92-64-05918-4 – © OECD 2009

Figure 6.7. **Dynamics of different influences on further education and skills training in the United Kingdom**

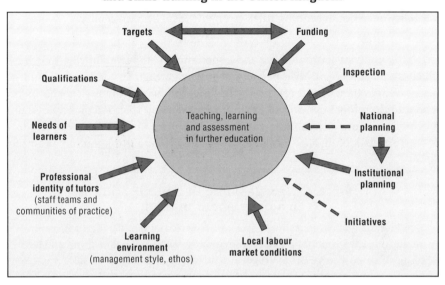

Source: Steer *et al.* (2006), "Modernisation and the Role of Policy Levers in the Learning and Skills Sector" presentation to BERA conference.

local in nature, and the other half are influences that are determined by national government policy levers.

However, it can be argued that the primary influences should be "local labour market conditions" (*i.e.* employer demand) and "needs of learners", both of which imply that planning is best conducted at a local level. The experience of the United Kingdom's Learning and Skills Council[1] in attempting to balance the demands of national targets and local needs has been a difficult one. Furthermore, the costs of maintaining local offices are high and there have been reductions in staffing and offices leading to a greater concentration on the regional level.

The key question for national governments arising from Figure 6.7 is whether the national policy levers are designed to empower local influences or whether they inhibit the effective transmission of employer and learner demands to the local planners and suppliers of training? How targets are set, and how funding is paid, are strong determinants of the extent of local discretion and flexibility that is permitted in any system. Amongst many factors, this balance is likely to be determined by the:

● Amount of trust between national and local.

● Perceived level of local capacity by national policy-makers.

● Urgency of national aims and objectives, especially the implementation of political manifesto commitments.

● Ability of national funding rules to enable local accountability.

● The institutional legacy of national agencies.

This analysis is reinforcing the experience of those countries that have taken steps to decentralise because it involves: high to medium risk; large institutional change; and reform of funding and accountability mechanisms. It should therefore be useful to explore when decentralisation of employment and skills is more or less important to an economy. Box 6.3 describes the role of decentralisation in New Zealand within a tight labour market, for example.

Box 6.3. **New Zealand: Decentralisation in a tight labour market**

Before the global economic slow down, New Zealand had a high performing labour market – economic and employment growth had been strong and had outperformed the OECD average. An unemployment rate of 3.8% and an employment rate of 78% brought real achievements – all regions have benefited and disparities have been reduced.

However, New Zealand has low labour productivity and widespread skill shortages. In addition net migration levels are reducing and the tight labour market added to wage pressures in the economy.

The New Zealand Government sets the policy framework and each region has an annual Regional Plan, co-ordinated by the Ministry of Social Development, which includes improving opportunities for working age people. More flexibility has been introduced to allow for local solutions to be devised and delivered.

There is now a clear policy and delivery framework incorporating the national, regional and local levels. The national level is responsible for policy, regulation, key services, developing public private partnerships. The regions cover strategic planning, developing and agreeing regional strategies, fostering regional partnerships. The local level has some flexibility in how it implements employment and training services and also has local partnerships.

Box 6.3. **New Zealand: Decentralisation
in a tight labour market** (*cont.*)

New Zealand is also stressing the integration of service delivery, especially between the public employment service and non-government agencies. At the same time it is improving co-ordination between, and within, government agencies. New Zealand's overall strategic themes for 2007 are: families young and old; economic transformation; and national identity. The priorities for economic transformation are:

● Increase sustainable employment.

● Infra-structure for growth.

● Raising capability and productivity.

● Changing economic profile.

The government has also established an industry partnership which gives a national forum for discussion with industry on social and economic matters and enables government to set out its "service offer" to partners.

National, regional, local institutions and industry are all involved in taking reforms forward. To meet the challenges in the labour market and wider social objectives, New Zealand is driving further integration within policy areas (employment, health, housing) and between them (economic, social and cultural).

Source: Barker and Smith (2008).

Indicators for when decentralisation is needed

It is useful to consider what sort of indicators there may be for when national strategic frameworks and programmes need to be reformed. The following may be considered:

● When the ratio between the unemployed and the working age economically inactive shifts strongly towards the inactive. Whilst there may be a number of reasons for such shifts (including administrative measures) it is an indication that long-term unemployment is being "hidden" by inactive or passive benefits.

● When there is a growing proportion of the workless who have multiple labour market disadvantages. National programmes and/or tighter conditionality can be highly effective at creaming off the most employable but they often leave behind those who have the lowest employability.

● When workless people become more geographically concentrated. There are complex inter-relationships between place, economy, and worklessness – often connected to housing policy. However, greater concentration of workless people can occur because of: former or continuing industrial re-structuring; concentrations of low-cost housing; and where neighbourhoods have become "detached" from the local economy for a variety of reasons.

- When national programmes have a declining success rate. Whilst there can be different reasons for declining performance, if this is linked with the above indicators it is likely that the national interventions are not providing what individuals and employers need.

- When there are an increasing proportion of returners on unemployment benefits. This is likely to be due to a combination of people with low employability not being able to sustain employment and changing labour market demand creating more temporary and insecure jobs. Economies with more flexible labour market conditions will be more susceptible to high levels of insecure employment.

- When there are significant variations in skill levels and declining employment rates for low skilled workers. This will be a strong indicator that certain local economies could be left behind within a growing national economy because of the pull of successful areas both for employers and higher skilled workers.

- When there are high levels of inward and outward migration. The push and pull factors for migration (both domestic and internationally) are highly varied, but the impact of inward and outward migration can result in dramatic changes to local economies – both positive and negative. Whilst migration may be the result of labour market adjustments at the macro-level, the consequences at the micro-level can be severe requiring state intervention of one kind or another.

- Finally, the question has to be asked that, if these indicators are all present, does this add up to a case for decentralising employment and skills? Most of the indicators could still be dealt with by national interventions, however the risk is that policy objectives and goals will be set in parallel by government departments leading to confusions and inefficiencies at the local level. This need not be the case if central government is committed to "joining up" across departments. There are recent examples in the United Kingdom of combining separate funds into a single "Working Neighbourhood Fund", as well as a more controversial linking of access to social housing with employment.

The core argument is that in periods of low or declining unemployment the position of the most disadvantaged people and areas becomes more visible to society and policy-makers. In terms of achieving wider social inclusion goals this is critical – it provides the chance to extend more opportunities to people and places that otherwise may not benefit.

The common themes that run through these indicators are that to tackle higher levels of disadvantage requires multi-faceted services to individuals and a stronger emphasis on place. Decentralisation therefore appears to be a necessary condition for joining up services at the point of delivery and for disadvantaged areas to put in place the solutions necessary to tackle their specific problems.

There are other approaches to decentralisation but these are not necessarily mutually exclusive. First, the responsiveness and flexibility of the public employment service and skills training infra-structure can be improved. Second, national frameworks using contractors to deliver "black box" provision could deliver more personalised services attuned to local needs. Delivering either of these approaches still requires a far higher degree of sensitivity to the local level – the public employment service needs to understand how to effectively use its increased flexibility and contractors will want to understand how they can improve outcomes in the local context.

Most forms of decentralisation involve some form of local partnership arrangements, but these take on a wide variety of different forms and functions. If the value of decentralisation is to be realised then local partnerships need to be designed to be "fit for purpose" and provide the potential for expanding their responsibilities.

Local partnership to improve delivery

Giguère (2005) summed up the potential of partnerships, but also highlighted the obstacles to effective partnership working:

> [P]artnership is a valuable tool. It can have a significant impact on local governance, as long as it is seen by the partners as a way to improve their action, not as a substitute for action. There are, however, a number of obstacles to this. Effective partnership working is impeded by: a) A disconnection between national policy objectives and local goals; this can happen even when national ministries set the goals for partnerships and are represented in the partnerships. b) The limited administrative flexibility of many public programmes, including those which are relevant to local economic and employment development. c) Weak accountability relationships, between the various partners, between the partnership and the public, and between the representatives and their constituency. And; d) a tendency for partnership-based organisations to be process-driven as they seek to secure their continuity.

To help overcome these obstacles the OECD (2001) made recommendations for how local partnerships can be improved:

- Make policy goals consistent at central level.
- Adapt the strategic framework for the partnership to the needs of the partners.

- Strengthen the accountability of partnerships.
- Provide flexibility in the management of public programmes.

These recommendations are still highly relevant and provide a useful structure for countries to evaluate their current arrangements. So far it has been argued that there are three key challenges to skills and employability systems:

- Increasing the adaptability of local workforce and therefore also of the supply-side infra-structure.
- Personalising services for people with a range of labour market barriers, as well as employability skills, to adapt to changing labour market conditions and jobs.
- Reducing the complexity of the institutional arrangements for policy, planning and delivery.

Using the OECD recommendations can help provide a focus on what can be done to meet each of these challenges.

Make policy goals consistent at central level

If one task of local partnerships is to reconcile competing or inconsistent national policy goals then improving consistency at the national level should lead to a stronger focus on delivery by local partnerships. It is a common complaint that the policy tensions at the national level (for example, between work-first and human capital advocates) are repeated at the local level, leading to more conflictual partnerships.

Identifying common national goals for the whole skills and employment infra-structure is therefore critical. Some countries have set employment rate goals, for example, Netherlands and the United Kingdom have both set an employment rate of 80% as a target or as a national aspiration. The advocates of this sort of goal argue that it drives the behaviour of policy makers at all levels. It requires answers to key questions, such as: Who needs to move into employment to attain 80%?; What are their characteristics and barriers to employment?; Where do they live?; What service reform is needed to meet targets?

For example, Figure 6.8 shows the existing divergence from an 80% employment rate for different ages and by gender in the United Kingdom. It shows that for men between the ages of 25 to 49 employment rates are already approaching 90%, so if an 80% employment rate is to be reached there needs to be a stronger concentration on older people, women (especially those returning to the labour market), and young people (although this has to be moderated by targets to increase participation in higher and further education).

The setting of a national employment rate goal starts the process of regions and local areas asking what their employment rate should be if the

Figure 6.8. **Employment rate shortfalls from 80% aspiration: Age and gender**

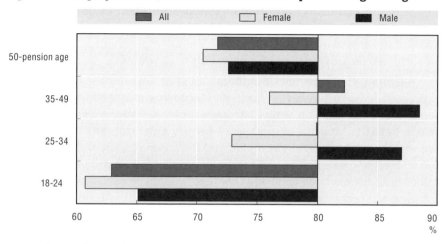

Source: Labour Market Statistics First Release (February 2009), Office for National Statistics.

country is to achieve the target. In the United Kingdom this is now part of a "Local Area Agreement" process which central government has with many local authorities along with their local strategic partnership.

A further driver for more integration is "sustainable employment" – providing people with the necessary qualifications, labour market experience, and employability aptitudes to maintain employment, as well as to progress in their career (Figure 6.9). Instead of systems being driven by just by job entries, the emphasis is changed to maintaining people in a job once they have made the transition from benefits to employment. A further step is to measure the wage progression a person makes once they are in sustained employment.

Figure 6.9. **The challenge: Sustainable employment and progression**

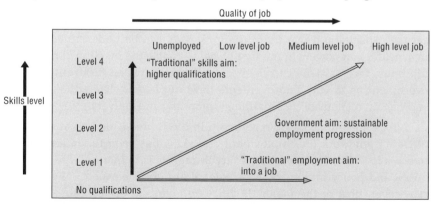

Source: Timms (2008).

There is yet to be any recognised definition of "sustainable employment" and different countries and programmes use different measurements of sustainability. The United Kingdom government has recently indicated that it wants to move to using 18 months of continuous employment as the measure for sustained employment and for payments to providers.

A United States review (Goldberg, 2005) of sustainable employment expressed it as "a person or family's employment situation provides a permanent and stable job, wages adequate for food, clothing, and shelter, full health benefits, and the opportunity for job advancement". This broad definition won't be generally accepted and the measurement of "a permanent and stable job" for skills and welfare programme purposes will vary. However, it does raise the question as to whether there should be further work done on defining sustainable employment and the principles to be used in its measurement to fit with labour market conditions?

Sustainable employment is an integrating driver between employment and skills services because it requires policy makers and service providers to think long-term about what an individual needs to remain successfully in employment. It has the potential to balance the work first *vs.* human capital debate by requiring both employability and skill interventions to be packaged for the individual.

In summary, national policy goals that set over-arching and consistent targets can provide a powerful driver to the whole system, and are more likely to be conducive to empowering local partnerships to also set ambitious local targets.

Adapting the strategic framework to improve local partnership

The intent behind this recommendation is to "enable public service officers and local officials to achieve their own policy objectives through participation in the partnership strategy. This will encourage them to use the partnership as a tool to improve the quality of their own action locally" (OECD, 2001).

However, the tension between different levels of governance can mean that the capacity and powers of the local level can be undermined (or they have insufficient powers in the first place) to enable the meeting of new, more ambitious, targets. This can lead to confusion between different levels of government as to why improvements have not been delivered, or a lack of clarity about responsibility for strategy, planning and delivery.

A recent example of an experiment in the United Kingdom to adapt the strategic framework for employment and skills has been the launch of City Strategies in 2007. The intention of City Strategies is to increase the extent of control and policy making by sub-regional and local partners. The selected areas cover most of the major UK cities and concentrate on those with the most stubborn problems of worklessness. City Strategies is based on the recognition that to improve welfare to work outcomes, local consortia are needed. City Strategies guidance states that "a central element is a new strategy to tackle the highly localised pockets of worklessness, poverty, low skills and poor health that can be found across the UK, many of them within major towns and cities".

City Strategies are based on the premise that local stakeholders can deliver improved performance if they combine and align their efforts behind shared priorities, and are given more freedom to innovate and to tailor services in response to local needs. This is a big step for the centrally driven Department for Work and Pensions and Jobcentre Plus (the public employment service), given that it has primarily tackled worklessness and benefit administration across the whole of the United Kingdom from a centralised structure. The then Secretary of State, John Hutton MP, described this as "a new contract between state and communities", pioneering modern forms of welfare delivery and offering freedom to innovate and flexibility. Speaking at the announcement, John Hutton said: "We are replacing the old one-size-fits-all welfare state that was run entirely from Whitehall, with tailored help for individuals and local initiatives. Harnessing the leadership our cities are providing will be a key part of this in years to come".

City Strategies is an opportunity to pool funding from multiple funding streams, and it is expected that consortia will join up the work of contractors, Jobcentre Plus and the Learning Skills Council to ensure that access to support is less complicated for individuals. Consortia will also be expected to ensure that the provision available better meets the needs of local employers, offering a clearer route from training and skills development to the workplace.

A central feature of City Strategies is to identify national regulations that pose a barrier to improved performance and then propose "enabling measures" to central government that will remove, or minimise the barrier. To date this has not been an entirely successful process; whilst cities have identified a wide range of enabling measures, the dialogue with central government has been difficult and slow. Many of these "enabling measures" have been focused on changes to benefit regulations which has meant that central government has had to consider the national implications of permitting, or experimenting with, variations. In addition, a common request from City Strategies has been for central government to share data on claimants, however this has proved to be difficult legally and in practice. However overall, the external challenge from the local level provokes new thinking and a deeper insight into the institutional and regulatory barriers faced by local partners.

City Strategies represents a further example of how OECD countries are experimenting with different frameworks to test how to maximise the integration of national and local policymaking. There appears to be an increased interest in how to make centralised systems more engaged with the local level, through a range of different mechanisms.

Whatever mechanisms countries may use, the principles appear to be the same:

- Frameworks should permit co-operation and not impede.
- Collaboration should be based on the achievement of mutually agreed goals.
- Goals should be based on an agreed strategy which in turn is based on a sound analysis of the local economy and the nature of local social and economic problems.
- Service delivery of different agencies should mutually enhance rather than undermine due to conflicting goals or institutional mechanisms.

Strengthen the accountability of partnerships

The need for national governments to maintain accountability to parliaments is seen as a major restriction on the ability to devolve. The OECD (2001) has suggested that local partners need to demonstrate they have clear policies and appropriate representation mechanisms with mandates. The more accountable local partnerships can be the more likely national government will devolve.

To tackle this issue among others, the United Kingdom Treasury established a "Review of Sub-National Economic Development and Regeneration" (2007) which sought to bring more clarity to the accountability and responsibilities of different partners and proposed steps to both devolve some functions and also to produce a more integrated framework between partners. In summary, it proposed:

- The possible creation of a statutory economic development duty on local government – this would require local authorities to carry out an assessment of the economic circumstances and challenges of their local economy.
- Ensure that Local Area Agreements (the set of indicators and targets agreed between central government and local authorities) include a clear focus on economic development and neighbourhood renewal.
- Reform current arrangements for neighbourhood renewal funding by more intensive targeting.
- Transfer responsibility for funding 14 to 19 year olds' skills policy from the Learning and Skills Council to local government.
- Regional Development Agencies[2] should play a more strategic role, delegating responsibility for funding to local authorities and sub-regions where possible.

It should be remembered that national governments control accountability mechanisms – the strength of local accountability is determined by the framework that government establishes. However, this may mean it takes longer to make the shift from a centralised system to a more devolved system because of the need to reform the responsibilities and accountability of different parts of the system. Structural reform need not hold up the task of reconciling the roles of national and local levels, and there are a number of methods being used to improve accountability:

- *Consultation:* requiring national government to take into account the needs of local areas in setting targets and designing national programmes.

- *Scrutiny:* giving powers to local partners to scrutinise and report on the performance of national programmes in their areas.

- *Challenge:* permitting local areas to identify national barriers and propose solutions.

- *Incremental responsibility:* devolving whenever possible where accountability risk is judged to be minimal.

- *Co-operation:* requiring local offices of national agencies to participate in local mechanisms and require active co-operation.

Creatively exploring the potential of these methods will lay the basis for increasing trust between levels of governance and between institutions. Increased trust combined with clear accountability lines can then create the conditions for new decentralisation.

Provide flexibility in the management of public programmes

The demand for more decentralisation and flexibility often comes from the local offices of national agencies. Local staff are often frustrated by their lack of ability to fully engage with local partners, share their expertise, and align their funding and programmes. This is one reason why the OECD (2001) suggests that national governments should address the need for "local public service offices to have more flexibility in the management of programmes [...] to ensure that their participation in the definition of a local joint strategy can be consistently followed up by involvement in its implementation".

OECD countries have explored a number of different ways to provide greater flexibility to the regional and local levels. Initially, it may have been accepted that some degree of local flexibility will bring improved performance but there has been mixed experiences when different models have been tried. Again, flexibility can be introduced in a number of different ways but the starting point has to be whether there is flexibility in the delivery of nationally designed programmes or whether flexibility is permitted in the design of programmes. The former can be carefully controlled and evaluated, whilst the latter involves a higher risk.

The OECD (see Chapter 2) is examining the extent of local flexibility permitted in labour market programmes and analysis shows that there is a wide variation in "effective decentralisation" across all member countries. Whilst these results are provisional, the OECD study is likely to provoke a new, and fruitful, way of how governments examine the shape and flexibility of their national infra-structure. It should also encourage local partners to focus their thinking on specific flexibilities that they wish to achieve.

So what are the possible steps that can be taken to increase the flexibility of programmes? Taking the elements of decentralisation used by the OECD in the study, there are some potential actions that could be taken to increase flexibility, as well as provide a fruitful area for the exchange of best practice:

- *Collaboration:* The extent of collaboration is governed by both local structures that allow or require participation and the attitude of the national agency to partnership. Strong and accountable local partnerships can lead to a duty to co-operate being placed on national agencies, for example, in the United Kingdom a "duty to co-operate" by Jobcentre Plus and the Learning and Skills Council is presently being introduced. If it is true that collaboration will be increasingly required then the trend will be to turn "voluntary collaboration" into more formal requirements to co-operate.

- *Outsourcing:* This is the area where much more needs to be understood. Most countries outsource part of their delivery infra-structure, so this raises the question of how markets for the delivery of programmes are regulated and planned. What role should local, sub-regional, and regional levels have in determining what is outsourced, the terms and process of commissioning, and the final awarding of contracts? There is a complex area but where some countries have extensive experience.

- *Design:* Greater involvement in design is critical for further steps in decentralisation to be taken. "Local solutions for local problems" implies that there needs to be a design capacity at the local level in response to distinct labour market problems. However, the capacity at the local level to identify problems and build solutions is not always present and governments would need to take steps to build this capacity.

- *Budgets:* There are a wide range of pressures on how countries construct and manage their budgets. As such major developments will probably be determined by other considerations, for example, budgeting to give individual customers more power. The use of individual accounts is intended to make systems more demand-driven and this will pose challenges to policymakers and providers alike. However, much can be done to understand more about the mechanisms that national governments use to fund activity at the local level,

FLEXIBLE POLICY FOR MORE AND BETTER JOBS – ISBN 978-92-64-05918-4 – © OECD 2009

for example, the requirements and conditions of funding streams, the targets that may be attached, how impact is measured, and so on.

- *Performance objectives:* Setting targets is inextricably linked to the national framework of goals and objectives. Cascading targets downwards from national objectives should form the glue that holds partners together in common objectives. However, too often there are conflicting targets that end up confusing providers and can drive organisational behaviour in the wrong way. The setting of performance objectives is one of the least decentralised elements, however what is potentially not recognised is that local partnerships can be more ambitious for their areas than nationally determined performance targets.

- *Eligibility criteria:* More control over eligibility is justified when there are sufficient differences in the supply of labour in local economies. Increasing local employment rates will be dependent on getting a different mix of unemployed and inactive people into employment. However, there is no flexibility in the majority of OECD countries, probably because eligibility is a rationing tool for restricted budgets. Furthermore, national ministries see themselves as defenders of the science around "deadweight" and "substitution" and believe that local pressures inevitably lead local partners to be more generous to individuals. Eligibility is an important management tool but it has to be seen as one element of clear local strategies and targets, indeed eligibility flexibility without a clear evidence-based strategy could be counter-productive.

Capacity of local partners

The capacity of regional and local partners to analyse their labour markets and devise strategies and programmes, remains generally insufficient. It is recognised as a significant barrier to securing more trust between levels of governance. Whilst many local areas can identify what they think is wrong with national programmes, they find it more difficult to identify the solutions. On the other hand, if there are experiments with decentralisation it can often lead to local partners being thrown in the deep end, with national offices waiting for them to fail.

There are some significant problems as a result of a lack of capacity:

- Labour market problems are not identified early enough and adjustments in programmes made too late.

- Systems remain more rigid than they should be.

- Well-intentioned local interventions but often inappropriate or ill-conceived.

- Inefficiency, reduced cost-effectiveness, and missed targets.

National investment strategies are needed both to build new capacity and to improve the performance of existing capacity. The key elements of such strategies would be:

- Professional competencies.
- Transfer of information and knowledge.
- Provider competencies.
- Inspection regimes.
- Market regulation that encourages investment.
- How competencies can be shared between organisations and agencies.

Finally, investment in capacity is more likely to be made by local partners if it is required to meet certain standards and/or targets. Lack of local capacity should not be used as a reason not to devolve, because capacity will usually follow a decision to devolve functions. However, it does have to be planned into the resources and timeline for devolution.

Conclusions: What more can be done?

This chapter has argued that adaptability of the workforce and local economies is critical to maintaining high levels of employment and opportunity. In a period of generally declining unemployment it has provided the chance to extend more opportunities to people and places that otherwise often miss the benefits of economic growth. Both economic and social justice objectives are met when countries have to redouble their efforts to up-skill citizens and attract into the labour market those who have been excluded before.

However, a constraint on improving adaptability is the ability of the state to adequately and quickly reform the delivery of training, welfare systems and employability programmes to meet new challenges. The characteristics of those who remain out of work have changed with significant numbers of people on inactive benefits and with multiple disadvantages.

This means that a greater emphasis needs to be placed on the *personalisation and localisation* of service design, planning, and delivery. Personalisation is needed to combine different forms of support required by people with multiple barriers, and localisation is needed to empower local partners to design interventions and direct resources to meet local employer needs and target the most deprived areas and people. Decentralisation appears to be a necessary condition for joining up services at the point of delivery and for disadvantaged areas to devise solutions to tackle their specific problems.

What steps can governments take to meet skills and employability challenges at the local level through better co-ordination of partners, and what can the OECD do to assist?

First, develop and test the notion of "decentralisation indicators" and, if linked with OECD research on flexibility, or "effective decentralisation", they could together be a useful tool for countries to assess and analyse the value of decentralising. There remains insufficient hard evidence to assist governments when taking decisions on decentralisation, consequently more sharing of research and analysis is needed.

Second, set consistent high-level goals on employment and skills that will drive welfare reform as well as public sector reform. How these high-level goals connect with regional and local targets and funding mechanisms is the task of strong frameworks that set out the roles of partners at different levels. The OECD could usefully research the different types of frameworks and their effectiveness.

Third, the role of local partnerships should be clearly established and should focus on: the extent to which they are consulted; their powers of scrutiny; their ability to challenge and propose flexibilities; the extent to which local partners are required to co-operate; and how they can take on increased responsibilities, but dependent on their capacity to do so.

Fourth, the inter-relationship between decentralisation and market-based solutions is potentially difficult and requires more research and policy development. Some policy-makers assume that they are distinct models, however some countries have successfully pursued both. The OECD can help describe and explain how these models can and do work together, and identify the role of local partnerships.

Fifth, building the capacity of regional and local partners should be led by a *national investment strategy* that identifies those capacities and skills that require improvement and ongoing support. The potential of decentralisation to improve performance will be maximised if regional and local partners are highly skilled at analysing needs, designing services, and delivering improvements. The OECD could help identify models for capacity building and, based on international experience, consider developing guidelines around competencies for decentralisation.

Finally, if unemployment continues to increase significantly as a result of the current economic slowdown then the case for decentralisation could be open to challenge as national governments re-orientate their policy priorities on managing the flow of unemployed claimants. Advocates for the benefits of decentralisation will have to remind policy-makers of the progress that has been made in recent years in many countries. The gains of reducing economic inactivity, continued welfare and skills reform, and providing better opportunities for disadvantaged people and places cannot afford to be lost.

Notes

1. England's funding body for further education, adult and community learning, and workplace learning. Scotland and Wales have devolved agencies with broadly the same responsibilities.

2. Regional Development Agencies in England are the government agencies responsible for the economic development of regions.

Bibliography

Barker, P. and M. Smith (2008), "Employment and Skills in a Tight Labour Market: the New Zealand Experience", presentation at the OECD Conference on Decentralisation and Co-ordination: The Twin Challenges of Labour Market Policy, Venice, 17-19 April 2008.

Cerexhe, B. (2008), "L'accord de coopération mobilité interrégionale: augmenter les possibilités d'embauche et les compétences d'emploi" (The Co-operation Agreement on Inter-regional Mobility: Increasing Job Opportunities and Competence Development), presentation at the OECD Conference on Decentralisation and Co-ordination: The Twin Challenges of Labour Market Policy, Venice, 17-19 April 2008.

Freud, D. (2007), "Reducing Dependency, Increasing Opportunity", UK Department for Work and Pensions, United Kingdom.

Giguère, S. (2005), "Local Employment Development, Decentralisation, Governance and the Role of Government", in S. Giguère and Y. Higuchi (eds.), Local Governance for Promoting Employment: Comparing the Performance of Japan and Seven Countries, Japan Institute for Labour Policy and Training (JILPT), Tokyo.

Goldberg, C. (2005), "Sustainable Employment: No Shortcuts to Living Wage Jobs", Research and Evaluation Brief, Vol. 4, Issue 7, Commonwealth Corporation, Boston.

Hasluck, C. and A.E. Green (2007), "What Works for Whom? A Review of Evidence and Meta-Analysis for the Department for Work and Pensions", Research Report No. 407, Department for Work and Pensions, Leeds.

HM Treasury (2007), Review of Sub-National Economic Development and Regeneration, UK HM Treasury, London.

Leitch, S. (2006), Prosperity for All in the Global Economy – World Class Skills, Leitch Review of Skills, HM Treasury, United Kingdom.

OECD (2001), Local Partnerships for Better Governance, OECD Publishing, Paris.

OECD (2007), Sickness, Disability and Work: Breaking the Barriers, Vol. 2, OECD Publishing, Paris.

Porter, M.E. and C.H.M. Ketels (2003), UK Competitiveness: Moving to the Next Stage, DTI Economics Paper No. 3, UK Department of Trade and Industry, London.

Serna Calvo, M. (2008), "Lessons and Challenges in Training, Skills and Employability: the Catalan Experience" presentation at the OECD Conference on Decentralisation and Co-ordination: The Twin Challenges of Labour Market Policy, Venice, 17-19 April 2008.

Steer, R., K. Spours, A. Hodgson, I. Finlay, F. Coffield, S. Edward and M. Gregson (2007), "'Modernisation' and the Role of Policy Levers in the Learning and Skills Sector", Journal of Vocational Education and Training, Vol. 59, No. 2, June 2007 , pp. 175-192(18).

Timms, S. (2008), "Integrating Employment and Skills: the British Experience", presentation at the OECD Conference on Decentralisation and Co-ordination: The Twin Challenges of Labour Market Policy, Venice, 17-19 April 2008.

ISBN 978-92-64-05918-4
Flexible Policy for More and Better Jobs
© OECD 2009

ANNEX A

Venice Action Statement on Enhancing Flexibility in the Management of Labour Market Policy

Ministero del Lavoro e
della Previdenza
Sociale

Local Economic and Employment Development
Développement économique et création d'emploi au niveau
local

Senato
della Repubblica

Decentralisation and Co-ordination:

The Twin Challenges of

Labour Market Policy

High-level conference organised by the Senate of the Republic,
the Ministry of Labour and Social Security, and the OECD LEED Programme,
in collaboration with Isfol and Italia Lavoro.

17-19 April 2008

Scuola Grande di S. Giovanni Evangelista
Campiello San Giovanni, San Polo, Venice

VENICE ACTION STATEMENT

I. Preamble

We, the participants of the high level conference on "*Decentralisation and Co-ordination: The Twin Challenges of Labour Market Policy*", held in Venice on 17-19 April 2008, propose the following action statement, which aims to underline the importance of enhancing flexibility in the management of labour market policy in order better to reconcile national and local goals.

At a time when human resources are so much at the heart of economic growth, it has become urgent to review the organisation of employment policy so that it is better able to respond to the opportunities and threats experienced by localities in a knowledge-based economy. Working together, we hope to make new advances on the critical issue of balancing national policy goals and local concerns in a way which reaps maximum benefits from globalisation.

II. Background: A Changing Role for Labour Market Policy

In a globalised economy, where both capital and labour are highly mobile and technology evolves rapidly, workforce development institutions have a key role to play in improving prosperity as well as working and living standards. Human resources are a fundamental source of economic development in a knowledge-based economy. Policy makers within the field of labour market policy and training have a major contribution to make, not only in providing the pool of skills which the economy needs locally, but also in fostering innovation, entrepreneurship and social cohesion.

The decentralisation which has taken place in many OECD countries in employment policy over the last 10 years has helped decision-making to occur closer to the "reality on the ground", but there is still some way to go before local labour market agencies have the capacity to make a significant contribution to broader local strategic goals. Achieving local objectives often requires cross-working between a number of different policy areas (such as employment, vocational training and economic development) to achieve integrated local strategies. This depends on the ability of local policy makers to better align their policies and services, which in turn depends on the *flexibility* they have to influence the delivery of policies and services. By providing such flexibility, national authorities can make it possible for local actors to work together on the complex and cross-cutting labour market issues which affect their particular community, to innovate as necessary and to adapt policies to local needs.

A major factor restricting the ability of national actors to make flexibility available in the management of labour market policy at the local level is the need to retain accountability. Indeed, this is one of the most difficult challenges faced by decentralised frameworks. Proper decentralisation implies a sharing of responsibility for decision-making at the local level among a number of actors, and agreement on an accountability framework politically acceptable to the various government levels. It requires partnership working among different stakeholders and between the national and local levels.

Capacity and intelligence are essential companions to flexibility at the local level. Co-ordinating labour market policy with economic development beyond the fulfilment of short-term business needs requires an understanding of both local and global economic conditions and an ability to help business managers avoid future bottlenecks, skills gaps and deficiencies in productivity. Joint and integrated planning requires locally-assembled data and expertise which can support the establishment of common strategic objectives and the better management of policy conflicts and trade-offs. Thus, for governments, building capacities and ensuring the availability of disaggregated data should also be central elements in any strategy to ensure the success of decentralisation.

III. Proposed Actions

We, the participants at the Venice high-level conference therefore invite national, regional and local level actors in the field of employment to work together with the aim to:

1. *Inject flexibility into the management of labour market policy.* It should be possible for the local level to give strategic orientations to the implementation of programmes. Local staff should have the ability to make decisions on the orientation of public programmes and services, in addition to achieving predetermined objectives.

2. *Establish an overarching management framework which embeds local flexibility.* Employment policy should be managed in a way which supports greater local differentiation while still paying attention to aggregate impacts at the national level. In particular, targets should be negotiated with the local level in order to ensure that they meet local strategic needs, while being embedded in a wider framework which ensures that aggregate national policy goals continue to be met.

3. *Build strategic capacity.* Enhancing local capacities becomes particularly important in this context, as strategies for human resources development must be integrated and matched to the economic reality on the ground. Staff within labour market agencies should have a strong knowledge of local business practices, local economic conditions, industry developments, and

appropriate methods to identify skills gaps and deficiencies in local economic sectors. They should also develop the analytical skills necessary to use this knowledge as a basis for developing broad strategic orientations locally.

4. **Build up local data and intelligence.** Building an understanding of economic and labour market conditions demands, as a prerequisite, refined data collection and analysis as well as expertise in a wide variety of fields. The capacity to gather data locally and organise it in a way which can support strategic planning exercises is critical. The national level can support this process by ensuring that data is disaggregated to the local level and by making available analytical tools which can be adapted to local circumstances.

5. **Improve governance mechanisms.** Labour market agencies should collaborate effectively with business, trade unions, civil society, education institutions, research centres, economic development agencies and local authorities. There is no governance mechanism which fits all institutional frameworks, but partnerships have a certain value in bringing different stakeholders together to develop appropriate and realistic strategies.

6. **Improve administrative processes.** Aligning policies through institutional reform such as decentralisation is a difficult challenge. In large countries, with complex distributions of power, a perfect match may always seem just beyond reach. A wide-scale review of how administrations function, co-operate and manage policies is required to support better collaboration between different administrative layers and between different policy institutions. This is particularly important given that the new, broader goals for human resources development cut across a number of different policy areas.

Box A.1. **Suggestions for a future agenda for the OECD LEED Directing Committee**

While some of the above mechanisms for change are already well understood – with a number of innovative examples of best practice being highlighted at the conference – more work needs to be done to help governments make the administrative changes and governance reforms necessary to meet this challenging policy agenda. The LEED Directing Committee is uniquely placed to look at these issues building on the collaboration with the Working Party on SMEs and Entrepreneurship and the Tourism Committee, which are also served by the Centre for Entrepreneurship, SMES and Local Development at the OECD. We encourage the OECD to continue its pioneering work in this domain, helping employment policy makers and other stakeholders to tackle the challenges and realise the opportunities associated with globalisation. In particular, we encourage the LEED Directing Committee, when planning its future work programme according to OECD rules and procedures, to consider the following issues:

- *Reconciling flexibility and accountability within labour market policy.* As noted above, a major factor restricting the ability of national actors to make flexibility available at the local level is the need to retain accountability within the delivery of policy. It is essential to develop new mechanisms to reconcile local flexibility with accountability in practice. Under what conditions would local stakeholders (labour market agencies, local authorities, economic development officials) *hold each other to account* in achieving success for their local communities?

- *Building better quality employment locally.* Meeting only short term business needs in economies with a low level of productivity may lead to high turnover, loss of skills, and poor economic development. In some localities, labour market institutions are working with businesses to improve local production processes and better harness the skills available locally, thereby leading to higher quality jobs and a more competitive local economy. What are the tools and instruments that prove particularly effective in this process?

- *Strengthening local strategic alliances.* Despite the "partnership fatigue" which is affecting many OECD countries, strategic alliances remain a crucial means of ensuring cross-sector collaboration, particularly when established at a local (sub-regional) level where economic development strategies are implemented. What incentives can be introduced to encourage effective team-working and problem-solving locally? What aspects of the management of sectoral policies and programmes most inhibit co-operative working?

> ## Box A.1. **Suggestions for a future agenda for the OECD LEED Directing Committee** (cont.)
>
> ● *Building local intelligence.* Data and expertise are required to support diagnosis and strategic planning exercises locally. What is the role of national statistical agencies, local labour market authorities and external consultants in building this intelligence? Should the tasks of developing labour market and business information be commissioned jointly by local stakeholders?
>
> ● *Capacity building.* There is a tradition of bureaucratic management in labour market administration which does not facilitate joint working and a constructive networking approach. It will be important for the LEED Programme to continue building capacities for labour market institutions to promote a management approach which is outward-looking, geared towards problem-solving within a longer-term perspective, and based on efficient consultation, cross-cutting collaborative work and peer reviewing.

OECD PUBLISHING, 2, rue André-Pascal, 75775 PARIS CEDEX 16
PRINTED IN FRANCE
(84 2009 02 1 P)   ISBN 978-92-64-05918-4   –   No. 56735   2009